CARPE PHONUM

How to seize the phone, take action and call your prospects,
even when you lack courage.

by Tammy Stanley

Carpe Phonum
How to seize the phone take action and call your prospects,
even when you lack courage
© 2006 Tammy Stanley
2nd Edition
© 2009 Tammy Stanley

Printed in the United States of America

Cover Design/Typesetting
Cathy Beard, BobCat Studios
www.bobcatstudios.com

Published by
T.S. Stanley LLC
Tempe, Arizona 85283
United States of America

ISBN-13: 978-0-9772006-0-3
ISBN-10: 0-9772006-0-4

Library of Congress Control Number: 2006908555

Dedication

I dedicate this book
to two women, who assisted
greatly in making this book
a reality.

Firstly, to my personal coach,
Tracy Quinton, who implanted the
idea by saying, "I just realized that you
are going to write a program called
Call Reluctance Reversed."

Secondly, to my dear friend,
Ellen François, who said,
"Tammy, 'seize the phone'—
why not call it Carpe Phonum."

Free Report:
3 Simple Secrets to Attracting
More Prospects

One of the biggest mistakes made by direct sales consultants is that
they don't know how to *advertise* their products effectively, yet they
rely on *word-of-mouth advertising* to generate leads and referrals.
In order to advertise themselves more effectively, they simply need
a better understanding of the critical marketing principles.

This free report gets direct sales consultants started on the right track
by showing just what is effective and what isn't, when it comes to
marketing one's product or service through word-of-mouth advertising.

> How to avoid the pitfalls most sales consultants fall into

> How to use the *Zeigarnik Effect* to increase your
prospect's interest

> How a Harvard psychologist changes your results on
the phone

Get this Free Report by visiting
www.tammystanley.com

Audio Products Designed Specifically for Direct Sales Consultants

To order visit www.tammystanley.com

End the frustration of leaving messages that seldom get returned

Leave Messages that Get Prospects and Customers to Call You Back

How to dramatically increase the percentage of prospects that return your calls:

> The question most consultants ask at the beginning of a phone call that puts prospects in a state of resistance
> The fastest way to get customers to disregard your messages
> The key ingredient of a powerful message that generates a return call

—————————————————————

You can dramatically improve your telephone skills

10 Keys to Sky Rocket Your Telephone Results

Learn the simple yet powerful strategies to skyrocketing your telephone results:

> How to avoid pushy salesman tactics and win with sincerity
> How to STOP making the mistakes that 95% of salespeople make on the phone
> The strategies and secrets that master salespeople use to get prospects in the palm of their hand
> The specific words that condition your prospects to say, "YES"

—————————————————————

Attention: Direct Sales Representatives Looking to STOP Postponements

How to Stop Postponements in the Home Party Business

Learn a system that shows how to assist every hostess to keep her commitment:

> The Secret to Stopping Cancellations
> Exactly how you get a hostess to keep her original commitment
> The top 7 secrets to coaching a hostess to do exactly what you want her to do
> How to expand your business with more guests and repeat hostesses

More Audio Products Available on Page 111

Contents

Acknowledgments

I have a deep appreciation for all people who have crossed my path, but certainly there are those who have impacted this work in particular. My husband, Jim Stanley, is at the top because his willingness to talk with me for hours and hours on end about spirituality, personal development, business, and current events keeps me continually inspired. Our four children, Marcus, Theresa, Audrey, and Zoë have been four of my greatest teachers – Marcus teaches me about confidence and undeniable loyalty, Theresa teaches me the power of tenacity, Audrey teaches me impeccable grace, and Zoë teaches me how to express Life with every aspect of one's being.

While in need of a graphic designer for this book, I asked that the right person be placed in front of me. Through a rather fascinating turn of events, I found that person – Cathy "Cat" Beard. Her design of my book cover and interior reflects amazing dedication, diligence, and unity.

I wish to thank my mother and acknowledge her for who she is. So many of my greatest strengths were exemplified by her.

I am deeply grateful to my brother Jim. As an English professor at the University of Pittsburgh, he has seeming little use for my book on overcoming sales call reluctance, yet his insights as to how to make this book more effective were invaluable. Thank you so much Jim for your acumen and inspiration.

To the many people who enriched my life during my direct sales career.

To my writing coach, Glenn Dietzel. He helped me break down the process of writing a book in a way that made it easier for me.

To a truly gifted personal coach, Tracy Quinton. She is the best at what she does!

To Miss Freda Dixon. Every single day her deep thinking, her intense passion, and her riveting instruction influence me.

Preface

Everyday all over the world sales professionals are waiting. What are they waiting for? They are waiting for the right time to call their prospects. No matter how much they visualize calling prospect after prospect on the drive to work, they quickly fall prey to a berating little voice that always suggests to keep waiting for seemingly good reasons:

 If you call too early in the morning, you'll be considered a noisome pest. Go get a cup of coffee and plan out your day. If you fail to plan, you know you're planning to fail.

 Better check your email before making any calls. You never know when an existing client might need assistance. You shouldn't keep existing clients waiting.

 It's almost time for the office meeting to start. If you get started on making calls now, you'll feel rushed. You won't have success with prospects if you're feeling rushed. They'll think you're rushing for the sale, and you'll lose the deal.

 People are getting ready to head out for lunch. No one wants to be bothered by a sales person, when he's getting ready to leave the office.

 People are just returning from lunch. They don't want to be bothered by a sales person, when they're trying to get settled in.

 Now would be a great time to call, if only you felt more confident in your script. If you don't feel confident, the results won't be worthwhile. There's no sense in putting time into making calls, if you aren't going to get the good results you desire. It would be more advantageous to get online and learn about effective sales calling techniques.

Calling certain prospects could really influence your business in a big way. When you've mastered the new techniques/ scripts you learned, you'll be able to advance very quickly. It's best to master those techniques before calling such influential prospects. You don't want to ruin your opportunities just because you weren't better prepared.

 You need to be really organized before you make those prospecting calls. After all, once you make all those calls you're going to have a host of new business. You had better organize your files and desk and put together an effective calling regimen.

 It's too late to call prospects. They're getting ready to leave work. Arrive here all the earlier tomorrow morning, and you can get all those calls completed before noon.

If any or all of those suggestions sound familiar, you probably know what it's like to hear a voice chastising you on your drive home from work because you didn't make the calls you were supposed to make. Strange, isn't it? It sounds quite like the voice that talked you out of making any of those calls all throughout the day.

Learning how to "seize the phone" requires investigating the voice that talks one out of making the necessary prospecting calls that advance anyone's sales business. There are plenty of programs to assist sales professionals become more efficient during the call, and certainly it's always beneficial to hone one's skills. But too many of the sales professionals I've met and clients I've worked with report that it isn't the sales process that trips them up — it's getting themselves to actually pick up the phone. There always seems to be a reason why it would be better to call later.

Most sales professionals understand on a gut level that waiting for a better time to call is only cheating them from further expanding their sales business today. But getting past a relentless, fear inflicting voice in their heads is no easy task. Of course, if it were, top sales professionals wouldn't be so desperately needed or so highly paid.

From my own sales experience, I've learned that the best time to call a prospect is as soon as I think about calling him. Waiting for a better time usually results in one of two things — never finding the right time to call that prospect, or waiting so long that by the time the call is finally placed, the prospect is already doing business with someone else and no longer requires the suggested product or service.

So how does one get oneself to the point that one can walk right past all those nagging reasons to wait and call later? In order to get sales professionals to "seize the phone," a process is required. I prefer to compare that process to a baseball player going up to bat, and naturally having the goal to hit the ball, run to each of the bases, and finally cross over the home plate and score.

Getting to first base involves coming face to face with the voice that talks one out of making all those calls. That voice must be presented, discussed and revealed as the liar that it is, before the sales professional can move on to second base.

Moving to second base requires learning how to detach oneself from the persistent voice that nags and distracts but never points one in the right direction. The sales professional needs a secret weapon that effectively dismantles the seeming hold that fear has on him, so he can move on to third base.

Getting one's feet firmly planted on third base occurs when the sales professional sees more to his business than the exchanging of goods and money. By opening his eyes to recognize the potential ongoing value he creates and the good that unfolds simply by contacting others on the telephone, he learns the greater aspects and opportunities of his business.

Finally, the sales professional must learn that getting to home plate is only accomplished when he takes his foot off of third base. He must come to grips with the fact that the sales process is a continual cycle, that everyday he must walk out of the dugout of fear, pick up a bat of immeasurable value, put himself in the game and start playing.

That is what this book is all about.

CARPE PHONUM™

How to seize the phone, take action and call your prospects,
even when you lack courage.

The Voice Inside Your Head

The Voice that Inspires You

There's a voice inside my head that inspires me and I'm betting you hear that same voice. Sometimes at night before I drift off to sleep, I feel excited by the new ideas and visions of success that I see coming my way. When these new ideas present themselves, the usual voice of devil's advocate must be absent because I never imagine any difficulties ahead. If anything, I feel more like a super power — capable of greatness and able to tackle any obstacle.

When you first conceptualize a goal, don't you feel excited? When you think of yourself actually doing something that you desire, whether it's taking a vacation to an exotic land, doubling your income, or getting physically fit, you are listening to a voice that inspires you.

My greatest source of inspiration comes from ideas. I believe ideas are divine. When a new idea is uncovered, I never cease to be amazed by its ability to energize and inspire. New ideas channel our motivation in new directions, which in turn rejuvenates us.

When we are feeling good about ourselves, we are like an open vessel and are most receptive to new ideas. This was clearly revealed to me numerous years ago, after I held several specific coaching sessions with the women in my sales unit. The format for the coaching session was a S.W.O.T., which stands for strengths, weaknesses, opportunities and threats. I requested that each woman share with me her strengths, her weaknesses, the opportunities she saw for herself, and the threats that kept her from experiencing all her opportunities.

After that process I noticed a fascinating relationship between the strengths and the weaknesses. The women, who described strengths such as being organized, sensitive, creative, and energetic, likewise reported weaknesses of being uptight, too sensitive, overcommitted, and likely to procrastinate respectively. Without fail, every weakness was born out of the strength.

Being very organized easily leads to being uptight about lack of order or structure. Sensitive people feel things so intensely that they can easily overreact. The creative mind gets so caught up in creating that being surrounded by incomplete projects is a natural pitfall. The highly energetic individual knows herself capable of maintaining that energy for long stretches of time, thus opening herself up to waiting until the final hours to take action on a project.

Recognizing this relationship between strengths and weaknesses, I began to view my own shortcomings much differently. Instead of being angry with myself over my irritating weaknesses, I began to focus on the strengths from which those weaknesses were born. When I focused on the strengths, my mind suddenly opened up to new ideas. Those new ideas fed my strengths and starved my weaknesses, allowing the strengths to expand and the weaknesses to dissipate.

As a sales manager in a direct sales organization, I had to attend several conferences every year. I had sales representatives throughout the United States, so these different conferences provided an opportunity to connect with the women from different states at the same time and in one location. Before going to any of these conferences, I always undertook numerous creative projects, in order to make the conference really special and instructional for the women in my sales unit. However, I kept repeating the same useless behavior over and over, conference after conference – I never thought of what I wanted to do, until a few days before the conference.

For numerous years and several times a year, I would go two to three days without rest, working like a mad woman to get everything ready for the conference. During those times I would berate myself for waiting until the last minute and not taking care of things sooner. I would swear to do things differently the next time. However, a few weeks before the next conference I wouldn't be able to think of anything that I normally did. I would know that I needed to be doing things, but I couldn't think of anything to do. Then, of course, a few days before the conference, ideas would come crashing in, and I'd be back on the same crazy treadmill of going without sleep to get everything done before leaving on the trip.

The last time that I madly prepared for a conference, I had learned that my weakness of procrastination was due to my strength of great energy and stamina. Instead of berating myself for waiting until the last minute, I kept telling myself, "It's okay, Tammy. You have incredible energy and stamina. You are an eleventh hour person, and you are going to get everything done before you get on that airplane." Little did I know, that positive approach was all I needed to open the padlock to ideas. One idea stuck like glue... as soon as you get on that plane, take out a notebook and write down everything you've done in the last four days. That's exactly what I did. Then I put that piece of paper in a folder entitled "Conference" in my filing cabinet. A few weeks before the next conference rolled around, I went to my filing cabinet, looked up "Conference," and had a list right in front of me of all the things I liked to do. I never waited until the last few days to get prepared again. Once I focused on my strengths of high energy and creativity, my weaknesses of procrastinating and being overwhelmed dissipated. Clearly, the voice that inspires us and guides us does not condemn us. Scolding isn't what motivates us to perk up and pay attention.

Years ago our middle daughter, Audrey, who was then just a toddler, would throw incredible fits when she was overtired. During those exasperating times, the most difficult part was convincing her that what she needed most was to go to bed. One day, it dawned on me to stop fighting her. While she was screaming and crying, I very quietly whispered in her ear to think back on all the times I taken good care of her. Then I reassured her that I knew what was good for her, and that a nap always made her feel better. Suddenly she stopped crying and screaming and calmly went off to bed. I never had that problem with her again. Anytime she was acting tired, I would calmly and quietly remind her that she only needed a little nap to feel better.

I asked Audrey a few years ago if she remembered any of that. She couldn't consciously remember any of it, but it was obvious from her behavior that the voice she trusted and responded to was a voice of loving support. Like Audrey, all of us heed and pay attention to a quiet and nurturing voice. Each one of us has a little child within who not only desires a calm and nurturing voice to lead it to fulfillment, it requires it.

The Voice that Sets Goals and Makes Plans

When you listen to a voice that inspires you, you naturally feel good and begin to design plans of action in your mind. Have you ever pictured yourself as the invincible sales person, able to leap to the top of the sales world in a single day? Have you ever entered an imaginary world in which the prospects never tell you no because you have all the right answers? In those moments, your success feels inevitable. There's probably no doubt in your mind that you are capable of greatness and that the world anticipates with pleasure the day you will burst on to the scene.

You are not alone. All you have to do is consider the world in which you live. So many of the things you use daily without thought regarding their origin are truly amazing inventions brought into manifestation from an idea in someone's mind. Surely Thomas Edison retreated into a visionary world where electricity could be harnessed to generate light. I feel certain he saw himself as a successful inventor over and over again in his mind's eye. How else could he tolerate the humiliation, or at least the disappointment, that surely accompanies any person who fails thousands of times before experiencing success?

The Voice that Sidetracks You

Here's what never ceases to amaze me. After spending a night thinking about the greatness of which I'm surely capable and devising a plan in which to demonstrate myself as such, I'll find myself the next day listening to a voice that keeps me busy doing anything and everything but the tasks that are important in order to achieve my goals.

Have you ever found yourself lying in bed and planning your next day's activities – envisioning all the prospects you'll call and having a full calendar of appointments by the end of the day? But the next morning, you go into your office to start making the calls only to hear a voice tell you that you should go make some coffee – that way you can at least enjoy a nice cup of coffee while making all those calls.

When you return to your office to start dialing those phone numbers, you hear a voice tell you how important it is to stay on top of that email; if a client is trying to contact you via email, you need to respond quickly. How can you argue with a voice that's trying to keep you in touch with your potential customers? Once you're done checking email, you know it's time to make those prospecting calls, but before you settle into making calls, you follow the suggestion of that little voice to go and check in with a few of the people in the office. After all, it would be rude to completely ignore your office associates!

On your way back to your office, you might hear a voice telling you that you should reward yourself for getting such a great start on the day. Here it is 10:00 a.m. and you've already answered email, you've checked in with all the people in the office, and you're going to be making all those calls today. Imagine listening to a voice that tells you to reward yourself because of all the calls you are going to make that day! Before you know it, you find yourself in the "break room" getting a cookie to enjoy with your coffee for a job that will be done in the future.

Of course, when you return to your office, that familiar voice tells you that you won't sound professional if you're drinking coffee and eating a cookie while you're talking to prospects. It is best to finish the cookie and the coffee while you do something else like read the newspaper. Hey, you have to stay on top of the news in your line of business! If you don't, you'll risk sounding like a fool who doesn't even know what's going on in the world. No sooner have you put that last bite of cookie into your mouth, you're sure to hear an all too familiar voice, "Cookies for breakfast? You were supposed to start a new diet today. How are you ever going to reach your goal of making all those calls, when you can't even stick to a diet for half a morning?"

By the time you've finished your coffee, you no longer feel ready to make all those calls. Somehow you don't really feel confident enough to talk to prospects. And everyone knows that there's no point in calling potential prospects, if you don't feel confident. You have to feel confident, or you'll just be wasting your time! Luckily that little voice is there to coach you and tell you just what you need to do now. This is the perfect time to go get that new book you just heard about, the one that reveals the secrets of master salespeople.

Whenever you accept the belief that you don't feel confident enough to make a sales call, you can be sure that little voice will sneak in and convince you to do something more important like organize your desk. After all, if you want to be successful, you must be really organized to handle all the business that will be coming your way, once you make those phone calls!

Too many sales people know what it's like to follow the suggestions of that little voice around all day long. It can definitely keep one very busy. However, at the end of the day, no real progress is made. Of course, those phone calls can always be done *tomorrow*.

The Voice that Blames You

If you're like most sales professionals, you go to bed at night having put in a full day's work, but you may not have made even one prospecting phone call. Are you then able to drift peacefully off to sleep? How can you, when a voice in your head chastises you for not following through with your original plans? Strange, isn't it? It sounds like the same voice you heard earlier during the day, the voice that continually suggested you do something other than make phone calls.

You're not alone. I know this because I often tell the story about a salesperson just like that. People come up to me afterwards and tell me they are certain I've been following them around during the day. I remember one woman asking me, "Oh my, how did you ever figure that out about people like me?" Isn't it funny how we feel we're the only ones who sabotage ourselves in a particular manner?

The Vicious Cycle of Self-Sabotage

One of my favorite movies is Groundhog Day because I can completely empathize with the main character. In the story, Phil, the weather man (played to possible perfection by Bill Murray) is trapped living the same day over and over and over again. He's not living the day he desires to live; he's stuck living a day he totally dreads – over and over again.

I know what it's like to experience that. For years, late at night in bed I dreamed of the life I would create tomorrow. When the morrow arrived, I followed the urgings of that little voice all day as it kept me busy doing task after task after task – almost none of which were on the list of actions that would create my true desire. I had planned the kind of day I wanted to experience, but I'd continually wake up and live the day I dreaded. I wanted so badly for that day to change, but I didn't believe I had the necessary courage to transform the predictable outcome.

You can find yourself in the same predicament, because it's so easy to think that the pestering voice you hear all day long is there to help coach and guide you. However, like me, you must face the insanity that comes from wanting desperately to achieve something and simultaneously avoiding any action toward it.

The Problem in Wanting a "Cure All"

I comforted myself by picturing the life I desired, the goals I had in mind to create that life, and by promising that I would get right to it first thing tomorrow. Although this went on for what seemed forever, and although I felt extremely worn out from the insanity of it all, I couldn't seem to stop the process. I just kept thinking of myself as weak and needing to learn some secret that others who were "more successful" must know about.

I continually looked for the magic audio tape series or the magic book that would hold the solution to ending the circle of sabotage in which I was ensconced. Every two weeks I was reading another self-help book or listening to still another tape of a motivational speaker. I felt certain that someday I would hear something that would magically change the process for me. I was looking for a very specific recipe – one that would make all my prospecting sales calls easy to make with a high percentage of good results.

It wasn't that I didn't see the vicious cycle to which I was harnessed. I not only saw it, I felt it. My body actually ached from the affliction of self-sabotage. I wanted a way out. But what I really wanted was a magic pill. Someone, somewhere had the "cure" and I had to find that someone.

What I didn't realize then was that as long as I kept looking for the cure outside myself, I would never find it. It reminded me of Dorothy's journey in "The Wizard of Oz." She always had the power to go back to Kansas, but that power would not reveal itself until she could believe it. All of her experiences on her journey through the Land of Oz culminated in self-discovery and self-belief. Like Dorothy, I had to learn that the way out was to look within myself for the answers I sought.

Getting Past that Nagging Little Voice To Obtain Your Desires

Pay Attention to What You Really Want to Do

One day while talking to my business coach, I grasped a new perspective. I was telling her about some people whom I had yet to inform about the clothing line that I sold. I told her that although I didn't want to call them, I needed to get over it and just do it. My coach then told me something that changed the course of my life. She said, "Tammy, you thought of it, so clearly, you *do* want to do it." The truth in those words seemed to resound in my entire body. Every night as I thought about the life I desired, I would think of all the people I could contact. The next day, when I avoided the telephone at all costs, the greatest cost was my heart's desire. I had tricked myself into thinking I didn't want to make those calls, but why would I have thought about making them, if I didn't really want to?

There was actually no logical reason why I would think of the people I desired to call, if I didn't truly desire to talk to them. *I never would have thought about doing something, if I didn't really want to do it.* I finally had a defense mechanism against the sneaky little voice that always talked me out of making my phone calls. Whenever it would lure me to the kitchen (obviously, I had a home business) to make coffee, I would say, "I said I was going to make calls, not coffee." When it would insist that I just mop the kitchen floor before making calls, I would say,

"Nope, if I've thought of making calls, that must be what I desire to do first; so I'm doing it FIRST!" When the little voice would tell me that I felt too nervous to talk to a certain prospect, I'd say, "Yes. I am nervous, but I thought of her, so I must truly want to call her."

Time after time I discovered that people were friendly and often extremely helpful to me. I didn't have success with every person I called, if a successful call is defined as one that generated a sale. However, I discovered I could feel 100% successful just by making the call now instead of later. If a potential customer told me she wasn't interested, I no longer had to waste time wondering if she was someone who would lead me to a booming sales business. Furthermore, I could go to bed at night and feel great that I had at least attempted to move toward my desires, whether or not I had achieved tangible results from any of the calls.

Who's Talking?

The first step for me was the understanding that I wouldn't think of ways in which to grow my business, if I didn't actually desire to grow my business. I had to become clear about who was talking. Instead of reacting every time I had a thought, I began to just observe the thoughts going on in my head. Then it became clear that most of the thoughts going through my head everyday were completely filled with nonsense.

When you resolve to observe instead of obey the thoughts passing through your mind, you take the first step toward freedom. This is the way to become detached from and understand the behavior that results from all those thoughts. In the detachment, you begin to comprehend that you have a choice *not to identify* with every thought you have.

I used to think that every thought that passed through my

head was my thought. Therefore, I took possession of each one. I owned them and lived according to them. When I began to observe without attachment, I felt as though I had suddenly become aware of an alien who was living inside of me and trying to completely take over my mind.

For example, I might be heading out for a meeting slightly behind schedule. Immediately these thoughts swarmed about − *how terrible it was for me to be running late; after all these years, wouldn't I ever learn to leave myself more time to get ready; people wouldn't think I'm professional; and people would be inconvenienced because I failed to plan with complete efficiency.*

For years I reacted to this voice. For years I felt guilty when I was running late for an appointment. Then I would get into my car feeling the pressure to hurry. Can you guess what I'd then do? Yes, I would speed like a maniac, filled with tension and anxiety, to my next appointment. However, the decision to simply observe my thinking but not react to it made me more impervious to its raging. Then I began to see how counterproductive it was.

The Nonsensical Solutions

When you're running late for an appointment, you feel a great deal of stress. The last thing you need to do is add to that stress by speeding down the road, worrying that a policeman is going to catch and fine you. Instead of spending twenty or thirty minutes of your time in total frustration because the lights are red instead of green and that others on the road are driving the speed limit instead of exceeding it, you can spend that time being immensely more productive.

By detaching from much of the thinking going on in your head, you can begin to understand this vicious cycle. The thoughts that steer you away from working on your goals during the day and then chastise you at night for not working on your goals are all fear-based. It is fear that nags about the evils of being late, that convinces you to feel badly for being late, and then suggests you break the law by speeding to eliminate the problem and therefore the guilt of being late. This thinking is worse than a horrible parent — it constantly rages, nags and gives advice, but it perpetuates itself even more, when you follow the advice it offers.

Stop Obeying That Sneaky Voice

The more you observe the thoughts going on in your head and the less you react to them, the more you'll notice that many of those thoughts have little, if anything, to do with what you really want. You might even feel as though someone else is putting ideas inside your head. That seeming someone else is often referred to as the false self. Yes, I am suggesting that what you always thought to be an integral part of yourself is in actuality a false self. To be successful you must no longer acquiesce to the suggestions of that false self. Indeed, you will uncover an amazing secret as you stop obeying whatever the false self advises. *When you stop following the suggestions of the false self, you discover how easy it is to accomplish everything you desire each day.*

Keep in mind, there is no pleasing the voice inside your head that rages on and on about all you haven't done or shouldn't do. Every time you listen to it, you allow that voice to become louder. That's why it's far better to ignore it and pay no heed to it's counsel.

Thus, I take my time getting ready, as if I'm ahead of schedule, when I'm running late for an appointment. Once I get into my car, I drive the speed limit, no matter how much the nagging voice bellows that I must hurry and not be late. Sometimes I pop one of those educational audio tapes into my car's cassette player and within moments I'm so engrossed in learning new ideas that it seems like I have just started driving, when I arrive at my destination. I relax and pay attention to the beautiful scenery around me as I listen and learn.

Every time I do this, my awareness is heightened. I notice how blessed I am to live in such a wonderful city. I also notice how most of the drivers around me are hurrying to change lanes and speeding, like I did previously. Instead of being angry with them, I remember the pain of that vicious cycle. Those drivers don't need my anger. They need some kind of blessing to get them through the rest of the day alive.

This may sound like I see myself as some saintly figure behind the wheel. Not at all. I'm a realist – driving the speed limit usually results in me being called a jerk, not a saint. However, it no longer matters what others are thinking, or what that nagging little voice in my head says. The experience of running late and driving across town in traffic even with numerous inconsiderate drivers is now something I can actually enjoy. A switch has occurred. Instead of a situation controlling me, I have learned how to control a situation. Recognizing the useless solutions of the false self has greatly assisted in doing the opposite of what it suggests.

Remember this secret: Refusing to do what that sneaky voice tries to tell you to do quiets its nagging and weakens its hold on you. And regarding the driving scenario, you're sure to notice something else – at some off-ramp stoplight, you'll invariably pull up next to a driver who sped past you miles before, proving once and for all that recklessly speeding across town doesn't get you to your appointments any faster than carefully driving the speed limit.

One of the things I openly admit is that I am a student of all of this and I feel certain I'll be a student of it for the rest of my life. Right about the time I start thinking "I'm the master," it becomes obvious that I still have much to learn.

Not long ago I awoke early one Saturday morning in order to be a judge for a Toastmaster contest. When I got on the freeway, I thought to myself, "I have a wonderful drive ahead of me. I'm going to enjoy myself and refuse to be upset by any discourteous driver." It couldn't have been more than five minutes later that I put my right hand turn signal on to move into the right hand lane. As soon as I turned on my signal, the driver in that lane seemed to speed up, as if to prevent me from moving over in front of him. I had to put on my brakes and let him pass by before I could move over into that lane.

During the process I could feel my blood pressure rise, as I yelled, "YOU JERK!" Seconds after yelling at him, I remembered my pledge from minutes before... "I refuse to be upset by any discourteous driver." I hadn't even stuck to the goal of having a wonderful drive for five minutes. Amazed that I could lose control of my focus so quickly, I returned to using a script that I'd learned in a book called, *Feelings Buried Alive Never Die* by Karol Truman. For a number of weeks I'd been using this script and gaining so many helpful insights. Its basic premise is that you locate the origin of your feelings or thoughts of anger, frustration, or hurt in order to release them and to choose new thought patterns and healing ideas.

By the time I had finished the process of saying the words in the script I'd memorized from Karol Truman's book, a wonderful new insight unfolded. How many times had I been driving in a car when I realized that I couldn't even remember a single stoplight or landmark from the time I'd left the house up until that point of conscious thought? And during those periods of time, when I was obviously immersed in my own thinking and driving on autopilot, couldn't it be possible that I had been oblivious to a driver with a turn signal on who was attempting to move into my lane? How quick I'd always been to assume that all the drivers making mistakes were a bunch of jerks. But perhaps many of them were people just like me, people immersed in their own thoughts, driving on autopilot, and unaware of the plans of the other drivers on the road.

When the false self is the tour guide, every road you pursue is a dead end street. There is no resolution within the false self, which is why you can feel trapped in the limitations of mediocrity and self-sabotage for what seems like an eternity. When you refuse to obey the false self and dare to oppose its counsel, you open yourself up to incredible possibilities.

Transform Your Behavior

The key to success is paying attention without giving in to the thinking that is going on inside your head. The false self plans its takeover when you least expect it. How many times do you happily go shopping, only to spend the time at the checkout bemoaning how slowly the cashier works or how slowly the line is moving? As you stand there, you tap your feet, you sigh, and you roll your eyes.

Exactly what purpose does that serve? Ah yes, it cues everyone that you're feeling irritated. And once you signal that loud and clear, doesn't the process always seem to take even longer? If the clerk is feeling rushed he's bound to make a mistake. If the clerk is doing her best, and you've let her know that isn't good enough for you, she's likely to slow down even more just to get back at you!

So, where did you get the idea to tap your feet, to roll your eyes and sigh? Did you really come up with that solution or did that sneaky false self come up with it? Look at the situation again. The line at the checkout stand is longer than you might wish. When you decide to stand in the line in spite of that, exactly how does tapping your feet make the line move faster? Clearly it doesn't. It's a ridiculous solution to the situation at hand. And the perpetrator of this behavior can be none other than the nagging voice of the false self.

Notice that I refrain from naming it "your" little voice. My reasoning for omitting "your" is that this isn't something you want to own. In addition to that, whenever I'm out in the public speaking about this, everyone in the audience is nodding his head or laughing. People relate to what I'm saying. They hear those same silly suggestions I hear. If we're all unique, how could our own *personal* little voice be giving us all the same suggestions? I maintain that we hear the same confounded suggestions from that nagging voice because it isn't personal; it's impersonal. And on top of that, it's a big fat liar! It attempts to make us believe that we are thinking what it says.

There's something incredibly freeing about standing in a long line and consciously deciding that you will wait patiently just because you really do want to stand there and buy those things more than you want to go home without them. One time I was standing in a line behind two women, who not only had loads of things on the counter, but in addition to that, they decided to divide everything into several separate purchases with separate receipts. The whole thing became amusing to me instead of irritating. I stood there *patiently* with a smile on my face; after all I felt like I was watching a comedy. When I finally was able to make my purchase, the clerk said, "I've never seen anyone be so patient. Today you're getting the special employee discount!"

By now you might be thinking, "I thought this was a book to overcome call reluctance! What's all this about patiently driving across town and standing in lines?" The point is to see how that sneaky little voice, that false self, never provides a useful suggestion. The sooner you begin to see that the better. When you see the lunacy in its suggestions and refuse to obey them, you find that you will not only overcome the reluctance to make a phone call, you will overcome any counterproductive habit you want to transform.

For example, most of us have ourselves convinced that we never gossip. If you were to be brutally honest with yourself, however, you'd find that seldom a day passes without experiencing some form of gossip. Sometimes it might be allowing, unchallenged, someone to say something unkind about another individual. Sometimes it might be adding information to a story already being told. But no matter how much or how little is said, if in any way you belittle another person without his/her knowledge, you are gossiping.

Contrary to popular belief there are not varying degrees of gossip. Any and all gossip is harmful. You know that to be true. Yet still, you participate. You believe that you don't gossip; yet you do. Why is it so difficult to face the truth in this matter? I believe it's difficult to admit because you know that you can't condemn others for gossiping about you, if you also gossip. Naturally, you don't desire for others to speak ill of you, so you convince yourself that you would never do such a thing.

If you don't like to think of yourself as a gossip, you can also infer that you don't want to gossip, yet still it continues to happen. This is because you fail to concentrate on what's really going on. As long as you mindlessly obey that false self, you'll feel very little control over the success of your personal and business life.

I finally decided to test myself — to see if I could truly classify myself as someone who didn't gossip. To my chagrin, I discovered that far too many times I added fuel to a fire, and it definitely pained me to see that. However, I always replayed the situation and I learned to ask myself this question, "What did I hope to benefit while speaking ill of another?" Every time I asked myself that question, the same answer surged from deep within — I had hoped to somehow feel better about myself.

I then began to ask myself, "Did it make me feel better, after I spoke unkindly of someone?" Again, every time the response came back the same — unequivocally no. I never felt better after partaking in gossip; indeed, I felt much worse. I felt worse because I had failed to acknowledge not only the best in that individual, but also her desire and ability to become her best. Ultimately, I believe that in refusing to acknowledge the best in another, we deny the best in ourselves as well.

Here's what I find interesting. As logical as this all sounds, it won't stop you from gossiping. Logic doesn't stop the false self. Most of us are so accustomed to doing whatever the false self suggests that we won't even recognize when we're gossiping. If we want to do a good job of designing our lives, we must be willing to face up to the times we mindlessly obey that false self. I remember once when I was with a small group of women who were gossiping about others. I was able to catch myself right in the middle of a sentence and think to myself, "Now Tammy, this is gossip." Then that sneaky little voice crept in and said, "But you can't stop in the middle of a sentence!" I had to really force myself to stop in the middle of that sentence. It wasn't easy, but I actually lived through it! And guess what? I learned that I could stop in the middle of whatever I was saying! No one said to me, "Hey, you stopped in the middle of your sentence. What were you saying?"

Stopping yourself in the middle of a sentence, and realizing that it's possible, is the same thing as catching yourself in the middle of an activity that isn't moving you toward your goals and dreams. You can stop yourself right in the middle of it. Leaving that break room after only taking one sip of your morning coffee and daring to let the rest of it to get cold, is a delightful way to tell that little voice that you're not going to listen to it anymore. You are making your prospect calls first!

Desire Is Your First Step

I believe the first step to anything is desire. We alter our behavior when we are responsible to ourselves. The root of the word responsible is respond. Thus, we must respond to ourselves. The way to stop sabotaging any business is to respond to the lack of activity that is going on. Learn to respond to the misleading suggestions of that little voice by doing the opposite of what it advises.

The journey to overcome call resistance requires responding to your behavior as well. Anytime you find yourself avoiding the phone to call the prospects you need to call, don't berate yourself. Simply remind yourself that you never would have thought of making those calls, if you didn't really want to. That always empowers you to stop listening to the prattling of a voice that suggests countless other activities, except the very one that takes you one step closer to your dreams and goals.

When you have goals that require altering certain behaviors in order for you to obtain those goals, you may become your own worst critic. I know what that's like only too well. I believe you have to learn to take things personally so that you face the truth about yourself and concentrate to learn what's really going on. This means to take things personal to the point that you willingly admit what you can improve. But I also believe it's important to avoid taking things to the point of being upset with yourself or others.

If I tell my husband that I don't like it when he drives so fast,

I appreciate it when he takes that personally and slows down. But I don't want him taking it so much to heart that I'm accused of thinking him not intelligent enough to drive a car. His intelligence and his capability to drive a car were never in question, just the speed he chose to drive. When you take things too personally, you often lose the lesson.

Finally, the best way to alter behavior is to never give up on yourself. Even when you desire to do something, you can catch yourself still listening to that sneaky little voice. It sometimes requires numerous occasions of observing yourself obeying that false self, until you can stop yourself *before* obeying it. Once you perfect the process, you must continue practicing it. Anytime you slip into old behavior, you have to remind yourself to practice the *right* behavior. We've all heard the old adage that practice makes perfect, but in actuality *perfect* practice makes perfect. Once we perfect something – that is the time to really get in there and practice it regularly!

It never ceases to amaze me how frequently I've fallen prey to obeying that silly little voice. Just the other day my husband, Jim, and I drove to the airport to pick up our youngest daughter who had just returned from a trip to Pittsburgh to visit my brother's family. We decided that the best thing would be to drop me off while Jim went to park the car.

After I got out of the car, my husband started to drive off before I had even shut the car door. The door hit my arm, as he started to drive away and it hurt a tiny bit. By the way I reacted, however, you'd think my arm got ripped off. I yelled at him and stormed off with my face tensed in anger. Within a few minutes I was able to see that I'd allowed that crazy false self to take over and convince me that my husband was a big mean jerk.

The truth is my husband would never deliberately do anything to hurt me. And I *know* that. So why did I react with such anger? It seems that for a few brief moments, I relinquished my true self for a false one. I had been fully in control of driving my behavior one moment, only to wake up and find myself in the back seat with a deranged twin now in the driver's seat controlling my actions. When you find yourself experiencing that kind of a scenario, remember the power in desire. Desire to truly understand what's going on, so your true self can respond, and you too can quickly replace that deranged twin at the wheel.

Perhaps the most powerful tip of all is to believe that no matter how much the false self insists that this will be humiliating and painful, it won't. The false self is just like a two year old throwing a tantrum – it needs attention more than it needs the thing it's screaming about. The only life the false self has is the life you give it by listening to it and following its shallow, useless advice. Pay no heed to the screams of the false self and you'll know first hand what it's like to open a door that once imprisoned you, even though it was never ever locked. Refuse to give the false self any life and you will finally be able to live yours.

The Secret Weapon -- Listen But Don't Obey

You must become a diligent listener. Listen to the thoughts going on inside your head. However, remember that listening to and acting on something are two different things.   Seek to distinguish one from the other.

For years I believed that every thought I had was my thought. Consequently, I took ownership of those thoughts and sabotaged myself from doing many of the things I wanted to do. If a thought said, "You don't feel confident making that call yet; do that later, after you've read a chapter in the latest and greatest self-help book," I believed that I needed to wait until later. If a thought said, "It's exasperating waiting in line. You could be doing other things right now. You're going crazy waiting for this clerk to move faster than a snail excreting rubber cement," I believed that I was going crazy waiting and that I needed to signal in some way that I felt completely frustrated.

Then it finally became clear. What if every thought isn't truly my thought? What if I act as a filter to those thoughts that aren't leading me anywhere but astray? When I began to distill the thoughts going on in my head, I noticed a pattern. Thoughts originating from the false self never cure the problem. What if you don't feel confident making a call right now? Waiting to make the call is only going to make you feel the same way for a longer period of time. It doesn't cure the problem; it only prolongs the problem.

What if you're in a terrible rush and you don't have time to stand in a line with the slowest clerk in history? Fueling your anxiety with thoughts of going crazy doesn't solve the problem. Leaving the store with the decision to buy those things at a more convenient time does. What if you have to get those things and you have to wait? Why not use that time in a constructive instead of a destructive manner? When I ceased my exasperation, I increased my creativity. I now have paper and pencil available to write down ideas. I always keep a new and interesting book in my car. If I arrive at the post office and there's a long line, I grab my book and educate myself while I wait for a clerk to assist me.

The false self is incapable of providing useful suggestions. Everything it suggests leaves you stuck with more of the same. If you are already frustrated with your situation right now, you'll only be more frustrated with it by listening to the false self talk.

I actually wanted to write this book for three years. I started several times before and I had quite of bit of writing in some old folders on my computer. Isn't it obvious why this book wasn't written three years sooner, when I first thought of it? I listened to the voice that told me I had too many other things I had to do right now; that I could finish this project when I *had* more time. Do you see how that suggestion would never solve the problem or fulfill the desire? I was never going to find time to write this book. I had to make it a priority above everything else.

I've always been in awe of people who invest the time to write a book. Why? Because I know that they couldn't possibly have the time to do that. I know that they focused on taking care of the important over the urgent. I know they were able to overcome the nagging of that sneaky little voice – the voice that always tells us to focus on the urgent things – cleaning off our desk, paying some bills, eating lunch, going grocery shopping, picking up our laundry from the cleaners, taking the kids to their lessons, cooking dinner, taking a shower, calling our best friend, taking a desperately needed coffee break to stay sane, etc. All those things are urgent, but they're not always important. A clean desk has yet to get even one sales appointment, whereas phone calls secure millions of sales appointments year after year. I have yet to read of a single incident in which someone died from skipping a coffee break. Even though my dry cleaner always asks for my number, he has never called me once and insisted that I pick up my clothing. I hope you get my point. It's not that you shouldn't take a coffee break, pick up your dry cleaning, call your best friend, cook dinner or take your children to their activities. Just be wary of constantly giving in to the urgent and failing to do what's important to you, namely, tasks that help you accomplish your goals.

Refusing to obey the voice that supplies dead-end solutions is a powerful secret weapon. When that voice says, "Go see what's inside the refrigerator," take a walk around the block instead. When it says, "You can take care of that later," just take care of it now instead of waiting for later. When it says, "You're overwhelmed with too much to do. You need to take a nap to get ready for all this work," make a list and start with the first thing you wrote down. When you've finished that, go to the next thing on the list.

One day my youngest daughter, Zoë, came home from school crying and moaning about her situation. She had too much homework. It was impossible to get it all done. I'll tell you honestly, she was in a state of hysterics. It seemed she was over-reacting, especially considering that she was in the fourth grade at the time. If you don't finish all your homework one day in fourth grade, how much impact will that have on the rest of your life? Clearly, none at all. But I could see that she didn't need a lecture, even if the message was, "Don't worry about fourth grade – no one cares about it in the long run." The only thing that mattered at that moment was that she cared. I could see that she felt it necessary to get it all done, but she didn't see any way that she could reach her goal.

Here's what happened (actually I've left out most of her hysteria):

> *I empathized, "You feel overworked."*
> *She cried even more, "YES!"*
> *"You don't think you can get everything done."*
> *She yelled, "I know I can't."*
> *"But you wish you knew a way."*
> *She began to soften, "Yes, but I know there isn't one."*
> *"There may not be, but the only way you'll know for sure*
>   *is to start."*
> *"But I have too much to do."*
> *"I believe you. Maybe you could start by just writing*
>   *everything down that you have to do. Then you'll see*
>   *all in one place exactly what you need to accomplish."*

"I know what I have to do, and I can't do it all."
"But could you just write it down? Would you be
willing to do that right now?"
"Okay."

After she wrote everything down, I suggested she begin with her favorite subject, even if she felt more pressure in another. Once she accomplished that, I suggested she go to the next thing on her list and to keep doing that until she was out of time. Do I need bother telling you the end result? Of course, she finished everything on her list. Imagine how powerful this was for her. I'll share with you that since that time she's come home on several occasions with loads of homework, but anytime she says that, I only have to say, "Well, just make a list, get started, and do what you can."

Look back on that conversation I had with Zoë. That's how I want you to deal with the false self. Let it rage, but don't let it convince you that you have to rage with it.

In my "Carpe Phonum" speech I begin with a great poem from Dr. Seuss', *I Had Trouble In Getting To Solla Solleu.* I suggest you take it to heart:

> *I learned there are troubles of more than one kind*
> *Some come from ahead and some come from behind.*
> *But I've bought a big bat. I'm all ready, you see.*
> *Now my troubles are going to have troubles with me.*

Perhaps the troubles that come from ahead and from behind are none other than the thoughts generated by the false self. At least, that's what I maintain. And in honor of Dr. Seuss' little poem, I call them "trouble thoughts."

In order to get past those trouble thoughts, you need a big bat. You need a big bat with which your troubles now have troubles. Doing the opposite of what the trouble thoughts say to do is your BIG BAT. This is the bat to pick up and use to get you past those trouble thoughts that keep getting in your way, so you can start obtaining your true desires. It is your secret weapon.

Why Courage Isn't The Answer

Why You Never Have Enough Courage

Haven't you ever thought of contacting someone you thought would love your product or service, but put it off to do later, when you felt you'd have more courage?   Of course that's one of the useless solutions the sneaky little voice gives you. Exactly how will another cup of coffee make you feel more confident? How will waiting until later make it easier?   How can reading another self-help book give you courage?   Those are all ideas generated from none other than those trouble thoughts, whose suggestions never direct you anywhere outside of a vicious circle.

The problem with waiting around until you have the courage is that you never do.   You can attend an incredible sales meeting, read an amazingly powerful book, or listen to an outstanding motivational speaker.   But the next day, as soon as you start to make that first phone call, certain trouble thoughts will try to convince you that you don't feel confident "enough" yet to make that call.

A good number of years ago, I saw a movie that shed some light regarding those moments, when we lack the confidence to follow through with our desires.   The name of the movie was "Three Kings."   The setting of the movie is in Saudi Arabia right at the end of the Desert Storm operation.   Several American foot soldiers and one of their officers cook up a scheme to get very rich very quickly.   The plan, although seemingly simple to complete has a flaw – it involves stealing – stealing a very large sum of gold from Saddam Hussein. Not surprisingly, everything doesn't go according to their simple plan. They experience some major setbacks, one of which being the Iraqis capture one of their soldiers. Fortunately they feel compelled to rescue him. Before proceeding with their plan, the youngest soldier asks his officer if they can go over the plan just one more time. The officer asks him, "Are you scared?" to which he replies, "Maybe." Then his officer affirms, "Here's how it works. You do the thing you're scared to do. You get the courage after you do it, not before." The young soldier argues, "That's dumb. It should be the other way around." His officer replies, "I know. That's the way it is."

Are you hesitating to pick up your telephone and make those calls because you feel you lack adequate courage? Did you buy this book with the hope that I would say something that would finally give you the confidence you need to feel comfortable making sales and prospecting calls? If so, I need to repeat that the courage, the confidence and the comfort all come *after* you make the calls, not before. Oh, I know. It should be the other way around. But that's the way it is.

Why Courage Is Never There When You Need It

The reason why you never have the courage when you think you need it is that you usually lack courage, when you're about to do something that you've never done before. Think about that. I remember when my mom bought me my first two-wheeler bike. It actually remained in the garage untouched for several weeks. I just didn't have the courage to try riding it. When I finally decided to give it a whirl, did I have enough courage? Absolutely not. I was petrified to try. But my desire to be like my older brother and my desire to have an easy way to get to school was greater than my lack of courage.

I was amazed how quickly I learned. In less than 15 minutes I was riding up and down the entire street. Isn't it obvious that I was never going to work up the courage to ride that two-wheeler until I gave it a try and learned just how easy it could be?

Indeed, riding my bike became such a delight that throughout my life I often depended on it as my mode of transportation. Do you think I ever felt I needed courage to ride it again? Of course not, right? Actually there did come a time when I was afraid to ride. Even though I rode my bike 30 miles a day during one phase of my life, I was only accustomed to city riding. The first time I went bike riding on a mountain road, I discovered that I became incredibly nervous. I wasn't used to riding on such small roads with steep cliffs on my side. I definitely didn't have the courage to do it. Once again, when I needed the courage, it wasn't there. Why? Because as much as I rode my bike, I had never gone up or down steep mountain hills on it before. Of course, I discovered the courage I needed after I rode my bike up and down and conquered that mountain.

Whenever you attempt something new, you'll lack the courage you need to do it. It actually makes perfect sense. How can you have courage to do what you've never done?

A number of years ago, I ran a really special incentive in my sales unit entitled "Take the Step You're Sure You Can't Take Incentive." I challenged my sales women to do something they didn't think they had the courage to do. It didn't have to be related to their sales business for them to earn a prize. What I wanted them to learn was the process. I wanted them to understand that we never have the courage to do what we've never done before. I also wanted them to experience how much unnecessary fear we build around that. One woman's story was such a perfect example and testimonial that I have to share it.

She had a habit of hiding behind the word "we." She'd say things like, "*We* need to clean this room," or "*We* need to get the lawn mower fixed." However, when she said things like that, she really meant, "I want *you* to clean up this room," or "I want you to go get the lawn mower fixed." She told me that the response she always received from her husband often frustrated her. Whenever she said, "*We* need to..." he usually responded with "No, *we* don't need that." It seemed he was being uncooperative.

Then one night, she and her husband were driving home and she was about to say, "We need to..." But she caught herself before she said it. She told me that she had to make the conscious decision to say the words she was too afraid to say. Then (probably after a deep breath) she said, "*I* really want to stop off at the store and get some ham and eggs for breakfast tomorrow." To her delight and amazement, her husband simply said, "Oh, okay."

I love that story. As soon as she accurately voiced what she wanted, her husband was completely cooperative. You too may feel afraid to say what you really mean or do what you want to do. However, you'll find that people prefer the real you, when you stop sugar coating your speech and say what you really mean to say. When you stop trying to please everyone, and for once decide to ask for what you want, you find that the world doesn't fall apart and most importantly, that you can get what you desire.

The Secret to Doing What You Don't Have the Courage to Do

The toughest part is probably moving forward and taking that step into the unknown — actually doing what you don't have the courage to do. How can you do this? You go ahead and do it, trembling and shaking inside and out, if necessary. That's the secret. When a trouble thought tells you that you're trembling, acknowledge that you are and keep moving forward. It's always going to be scary taking a step in a new direction.

Even though I've made hundreds of calls in my sales career, I still lack the courage to call new prospects because as much as I've talked to other prospects, I haven't spoken to the new ones I'm about to call. Experience shows me that I have no reason to fear making those calls. But every time I'm about to call someone I've never called before, I can sense that I lack the courage. What do I do? I take a deep breath and dial the phone number with my fingers trembling and shaking.

How You Wait For the Right Time

Have you ever found yourself waiting for the right time to make a sales call? Of course a trouble thought is the culprit behind this thinking. "You can't call now, it's too early." "You can't call now, he'll be right in the middle of working, and you'll distract him." "You can't call now, she's getting ready to go to lunch." "You can't call now, it's lunch time." "You can't call now, she's just come back from lunch and doesn't want to be disturbed by a sales person." "You can't call now, it's too late." You can wait and wait for the perfect time to call.

When I was in 5th grade, I remember watching Frank Shorter complete the marathon in the Olympics. I can re-experience the feelings I felt then by just thinking about it. You see, I was so amazed that anyone could run so far (26.2 miles) and so quickly. I had goose bumps watching him run his final lap. That same day I thought to myself, "Someday, I want to run a marathon." I had that same thought for 27 years. Each year I kept thinking, some year I want to run a marathon. But it was never the right time. I was too busy with school. I was too busy with babies. I was too busy with family. I was too busy with work. I waited and waited for the perfect time to train for and run a marathon.

Why There Is No Perfect Time to Wait For

The reason why there is no perfect time to wait for is that you must want to do it right now, if you thought of doing it. The whole point behind doing what you are sure you *can't* is that you are never going to reach a point where you feel like you can. That's the beauty of it. You don't need to wait any longer for the courage to do something because you're never going to get the courage until after you've done it anyway.

Anytime you hear a voice telling you to wait until later when you have more courage, when you have more time, when you have more energy, when you have more enthusiasm, etc., you have to wake yourself up. Wake up and listen to who's talking. Are these really your thoughts or are they those sneaky trouble thoughts that come from ahead and behind? Wake up and remember that waiting never changes the future. The future only changes when you stop waiting and take action now!

In 1999, I finally faced the fact that I had talked about my desire to run a marathon for 27 years. I'd actually never even taken one step toward that desire until the day I finally made the decision to act. While at a conference a few days later, I asked one of my fellow sales associates how she trained to run all the marathons she had run. She shared with me her training regimen. The next day I went out for a 2 mile run.

When I returned home from the conference, I went to the gym and I saw a sign about a club called Portland Fit that trained anyone to run a marathon in just 6 months! I'm certain that I never would have noticed that sign if I hadn't taken the first step toward my goal. We notice the things that are relevant to us.

When I lived in Germany for a year and a half during my college days, I can remember learning a new word and thinking how exciting it was going to be when I would hear someone use it in a sentence. You probably already know what happened. I'd hear that word at least twenty times that very day. I remember thinking, "Oh my, that word is used constantly. How could I never notice it being used before?" I never heard it being used because it wasn't relevant to me. Once I learned the new word, I was ready to hear it and use it. Until I was ready for it, I didn't even notice it.

When you put yourself in a waiting mode, you won't even notice the things that could be incredibly useful and meaningful to you. By taking action now, you open yourself up to new ideas and opportunities to help you achieve your desires.

My husband writes computer code and he knows how overwhelming things can appear before he gets started. He says, "You create analysis paralysis when you try to figure out everything that you'll have to do." He says that he's able to keep himself continually moving forward by thinking only of little tasks that might take fifteen to thirty minutes. When he thinks in terms of small increments, he's able to get started right away. Once he gets started on one idea and completes it, the next is supplied and then the next and so forth. It never ceases to amaze me how much computer code he continually produces. If he waited until he had the energy to write, he would never get energized. The energy comes after he gets started, just like the courage comes after we do what we were too afraid to do.

Haven't you ever come home from a long day thinking that all you wanted to do was zone out on the couch? To your chagrin, however, there's some event that you feel obligated to attend. You think you have no energy for it, but after you arrive and meet a few people, you feel like you've just received a second wind. This happens to me at night, when I go into my office to work after saying "goodnight" to our children. Many times I feel exhausted, but once I get started on a project, I suddenly uncover a burst of energy I never would have believed existed. There never will be a perfect time to wait for. The perfect time is always now. If you're brushing your teeth and you get the idea to put a particular thing in your car before heading out to work, do not listen to a trouble thought that suggests, "Oh, you can do that later, once you're downstairs packing the car." When you get the idea to do it, just go do it, right now.

Quite a number of years ago a business partner and I rented a rather large home together in the mountains of Colorado, and we operated a home daycare in that location. One of our clients was a senior flight attendant who desired a special situation. She wanted someone to watch her children in her home for five days every month while she was out of town flying with the airline she worked for. My business partner was the one who always stayed at the flight attendant's home. I never had any reason to go check on things there as my business partner managed everything that family needed, while I managed the needs of our other families at our business location.

However, one day there was some reason that I needed to stop off to help out. I don't remember what the situation was. I only remember my business partner and two of the three kids walking me out to my car, when it was time for me to leave. I was the last one leaving the house and normally I would have just left the door open, since they'd all be going back inside very soon. However, I remembered how much my business partner always nagged me about my habit of leaving doors open. Upon closing the door, I thought, "For once, she's not going to hassle me." Right after I shut the door, my business partner whipped around and sternly said, "You didn't close that door, did you? That door locks itself automatically and I don't have the key."

We suddenly had an emergency situation; a pan of hamburger was frying on the electric stove and the youngest child was inside taking a nap. Fortunately a locksmith came to our aid very quickly. The most interesting thing about this story, however, happened before I stopped off at the house that day. That morning while getting breakfast, my business partner heard a suggestion in her mind to put her keys in her pocket. She could not understand why she would think of such a thing. There was no need for her to have the keys. Whenever she left the house with the kids, they left through the garage. Instead of obeying the voice that told her to act now, she resisted. If she had taken action, when she heard that idea instead of listening to the voice that the idea was senseless, we never would have been locked out of the house that afternoon.

That story presents the problem we all face — how to tell the difference between our inner thoughts and those trouble thoughts. It's really not that difficult, once you follow the suggestion of truly listening before reacting. Once you're used to the dialogue that goes on inside you, you begin to notice the patterns of those trouble thoughts. You'll be shocked to learn how often they talk you out of doing what you thought of doing. Just like my business partner thought of putting her keys in her pocket that fateful morning, but a trouble thought talked her out of doing it.

That experience convinced me that we all have a calm and quiet inner voice that knows what we want and can guide us along the way. A key point to remember is that your true inner voice knows what you want. It's critical that you take action when you hear what you want to do. If you wait to do it later, you won't do it. Why? Because only a trouble thought can reason that you need to wait for a better time to do what you want. Grasp this now — **there is no perfect time to wait for.** The perfect time to do something you just thought about doing is always right now.

One day I was driving to pick up my youngest daughter from kindergarten and I was flipping through the different radio stations. I didn't understand why I stopped at the country station until I heard a woman sing these lyrics:

The secret of life is getting up early
The secret of life is staying up late
The secret of life is to be in no hurry
The secret of life is don't wait!

When I stopped waiting to train for a marathon and actually began the training process, something magical happened. I not only discovered a group of people who helped to train me in a safe and enjoyable manner, I discovered the difference between wishing and doing. I learned firsthand that after taking that first step, the next step is revealed because you are truly ready to act on it. I learned how quickly I could accomplish a dream. Just seven months after I began a training program, I ran the Portland marathon. After I took the first step of action, almost magically, the following steps became clear, as I needed them. I stopped a 27 year long ache in my heart in a mere 7 months because I stopped waiting for the perfect time. I don't know about you, but I find that far more impressive than running a marathon.

Value – The Unexpected Outcome

On the Other Side of Resistance

Every time you take a step into the unknown, you're bound to discover wonderful beauty and joy awaiting you. One of my favorite stories of the beauty we discover in the unknown developed right after we moved to Arizona in 1999. I had owned my own business through a direct sales company since 1992, and I had sales representatives in numerous states, but all my personal customers were in the greater Portland area, where I'd started that business. When our family moved to Tempe, Arizona, I no longer had a network of people who knew me. In order to get my sales business up and moving, I needed to network with people right away.

I found that the best way for me to do that was to tell people right after meeting them about the product I sold, as opposed to waiting and waiting for the right time. After meeting the teachers each of my daughters would have at an open house night, I naturally thought of networking with each of them. There wasn't time to talk to them that night, but I decided to go the school the next day and let each of them know about my business and the product I sold, that I believed would be beneficial to them.

In order to do that, I had to physically go down to the elementary school and invite each of those teachers to one of my sales presentations. I didn't have their phone numbers, so I couldn't call them. I had to walk into that school, hardly knowing those teachers, tell them about my business, and ask whether or not they'd like to attend a sales presentation. Since I was brand new to the school, I felt really nervous about doing that. Believe me, I didn't feel I had the courage to do it. I proceeded because I remembered that I never would have even thought about doing it, if I didn't really want to, and so I did it, while trembling and shaking inside and out. As it turned out, only Audrey's teacher came to the sales presentation.

I felt fairly good about that result, but the following week my personal business coach, Tracy Quinton, helped me to feel great about it by changing my perspective. She asked me what those teachers might have gained from me inviting them to the presentation. At first my focus was just on my sales presentation, so I expressed that they could have gained knowledge about the product I sold and its benefits, which was certainly a valuable thing to know.

Tracy's silence inspired me to look deeper, beyond the sales presentation and the knowledge that would be gained from it alone. I realized that those teachers gained the knowledge that I thought them important enough to invite. I had created value. Tracy then chimed in and told me that I would be the one those teachers would think of if they ever needed any help at the school. She was right. A couple of weeks later, Zoë's teacher picked her to be the student council representative for her classroom and asked me to be the room parent. I have to tell you, I was just as excited about Zoë's teacher asking me to be her room parent as I was about Audrey's teacher coming to the sales presentation. Okay, truth be told, maybe even a tiny bit more.

My first major task was to host the first grade Halloween party. Does life get more fun than that? A few days before the big event, I thought to myself, "Oh, I need to come up with a costume." I'd been Peter Pan so many times (I know what it's like to never want to grow up!) that I decided to step completely outside my comfort zone and be something scary and ugly, like a witch. I put together a costume and dressed up to see how it would look. Everything was great except that I just didn't look very scary or ugly. I looked more like Mrs. Stanley in a black dress trying to look like a witch. I asked myself, "What purpose will this serve if I'm not convincing as a witch?" That question kicked my brain into gear. Within minutes, new ideas as to how to look like an ugly old witch emerged. I changed some parts of my costume and when I looked in the mirror, I couldn't believe the transformation that had taken place. I could hardly wait for the party day.

Once the party time arrived, I drove to the school. As my car approached the school, I noticed something really strange. None of the other parents, who were walking up to the school, were in costume. I was the only one. Suddenly I felt frozen in embarrassment and fear. How could I walk in there dressed up as an incredibly ugly witch without any support from the other parents? This costume wasn't a little Peter Pan tunic; it was over the top! I hope by now you know how I walked into that school. I remembered that I thought of it, so I somehow must really want to do it. And of course, I took a deep breath and walked in trembling and shaking.

When I walked into the classroom, all of the children dropped their jaws. In a cranky old voice, I told them, "Mrs. Stanley couldn't be here today. She sent me instead. My name is Wanda, and that's because I can turn you into a toad whenever I wanda!" One little girl in the front row shriveled up into her chair. I realized then, "Oops. I've gone too far." So I turned to the little girl and said, "Don't be afraid of me, little girl. I may be ugly, I may have bad teeth, but I've brought you games to play and treats to eat today!" Suddenly, we couldn't keep the children in their seats. They all wanted to come up and talk to Wanda.

Throughout the party, the children kept asking me questions that would end up revealing my true identity. One little boy asked, "Are you Zoë's mom?" Wanda retorted, "Do I look like Zoë?" He said, "No." Then Wanda asked, "Then how do you figure I can be her mom, kid?" Days later when I returned to the school (this time as Mrs. Stanley), the children were still asking whose parent it was at that Halloween party. One little girl named Elizabeth came up to me and told me, "I know it was you. You smell the same."

Can you imagine the unexpected joy and beauty I experienced in that moment and every time I think of it? There's something incredibly beautiful about a little girl, who loved Wanda so much, that she memorized her smell.

We all know how quickly news can travel. A few days after the party at the school, I received a call from the parent of one of Audrey's friends. She had heard about my performance in the first grade classroom, and she wanted me to come dressed up as Wanda to her daughter's birthday party. At that party, one of the relatives couldn't get over my witch act and kept telling me that I should dress up as Wanda and entertain people at parties. When she said, "Tammy, people will pay you to come to their parties," that triggered my brain with a new idea. I didn't want to entertain at people's parties, but I did envision how fun it would be to design a sales training with Wanda the Witch as the sales trainer. A few months after that, Wanda was loose in the community, speaking at meetings and events, just as I had envisioned.

Every time Wanda goes out to speak, I guarantee you, it's risky. Sometimes the audience's response is lukewarm (which is definitely not the response Wanda seeks), but most of the time the response is lively and highly enthusiastic. So many people have told me that Wanda says things in a manner that stays with them and keeps them on track.

Wanda also made numerous appearances at that elementary school where she first began her career. Eventually the children figured out whose parent had dared to dress up and act like a witch. Now when I show up at the middle school, many of those boys and girls remember me from their elementary school days and approach me to say hello and ask how I'm doing. Consider all the ongoing value that has developed from something I did years ago. If you recall the beginning of this entire story, I went to the school to invite a few teachers to a sales presentation! Obviously, much more than "selling" developed from taking the step to invite those teachers to my presentation. I believe that is the wonderfully unexpected outcome from being a sales professional – the future value that comes from your efforts is untold.

Once after one of my sales presentations, one of my hostesses shared the story of the day her husband passed on. She said that the night before he died he asked her, seemingly out of the blue, to promise him that she'd stay busy if anything should ever happen to him. She thought it so silly for him to ask for such a promise since he hadn't been ill at all and showed no signs of any illness. But she obliged him by promising that she would. The very next day she received a phone call to hurry to the hospital; her husband had been taken to the emergency room.

When she arrived, he was in a coma and the doctor told her to tell her husband what she needed to tell him. She went to his side and told him that they'd been through so many things together and they could certainly get through this. Then the doctor said, "No, I mean I need you to tell him what you want to say before he passes on." Realizing that she was expected to give her final good-byes, she told him how much she loved him, how much she'd cherished their life together, but also how she'd continue without him and stay busy. In that second, he woke up out of the coma and looked at her with such intensity that she can still physically remember what that love felt like. Then, moments later, he passed on.

On the drive home after that sales presentation, I reflected on the story my hostess had shared with me, and I realized how it had deepened my understanding of love, strengthened my faith, and richly rejuvenated my soul. Apparently in some way I had touched her life enough to motivate her to touch mine. I find myself continually grateful for the story she shared with me and part of the value I hold as this — the sales profession will never be just about selling things. It provides the incredible opportunity to touch someone else's life.

When we touch another life, we create value. When we approach our sales business as an opportunity to touch lives and create value, whether or not the interaction ends in a sale, we find that incredible good and fun unfold in making someone else feel important. By keeping our focus on creating value, the telephone can become a very friendly tool through which we not only improve our business, but we also enrich our life and lives of others.

The trembling and shaking we go through to take a step into the unknown is well worth the value we find on the other side. So often we think we have to plan every step along the way before we can begin a journey. This is not true. We only need to start. Once we take that first step, the next one we need to take is revealed. When we learn to do what we truly "Wanda," when we learn to stop listening to a voice that tries to talk us out of doing what we really do want to do, we gain the opportunity to create incredible value.

How You and a Widow Share the Same Story

Translating each moment of our day to create a new sense of value is powerful. But I've discovered that many people involved in the sales profession feel stuck, especially when they entertain the thought that others are likely to view them as a pushy salesperson. So many salespeople worry about being perceived as pushy that they fail to do what's necessary to even qualify themselves as a sales professional, namely, pick up the telephone and call a prospect.

We've all heard the saying, "When the student is ready, the teacher will appear." Recently I witnessed myself becoming that willing student. Although I'd heard a certain story dozens of times, I finally was ready to let it teach me. Whether you interpret the story literally or as literature, the wonderful truth wrapped within it can quickly enhance your ability to tell everyone about your product or service without the fear of being a pushy sales person.

After the death of her husband, a widow finds herself in a difficult state – creditors are pounding at her door threatening to take away her sons as slaves. Her husband has died, leaving her without money and during this particular time period in history, women did not have an opportunity to earn a living.

Seeing herself in need of help, she goes to see Elisha, the wisest man she knows. When she tells him of her plight, he responds by saying, "What shall I do for you? Tell me, what hast thou in the house?" The widow tells him that she has nothing save a pot of oil. Elisha then instructs her to borrow empty vessels from her neighbors and fill the vessels with her oil.

So the widow borrows vessels and fills all of them *without depleting her oil*. Elisha then instructs her to sell the vessels of oil, pay off her debts and live from the profits.

Here's what inspired me tremendously from this story. When the widow first goes to Elisha, he neither *promises* her anything nor *gives* her anything. Instead he asks her, "What hast *thou* in the house?" The word "house" is often a symbolic word for "consciousness."

This is the point in which the widow's story becomes every human's story. No person, no matter how wise, can promise you or give you the freedom you deeply and secretly desire. You find fulfillment by asking yourself, "What is in my consciousness? What special 'oil' do I possess?" Understand that who you are and how you express the talents within you is your "oil." It is precious and has great value because your expression of you and your talents is unique to you alone.

Like the empty vessels waiting to be filled, there are people who want to receive what you have to give. Your job then is to sort out and find the people who want the precious oil you have to offer. You simply fill the void that asks for you to fill its emptiness. It's easy to think that your job consists of networking, meeting new potential customers, changing those potential customers into existing customers, developing existing customers into referral machines, etc. No wonder you feel overwhelmed, tired and even off track.

When you freely give and share your talents (your oil) you cannot deplete them. Indeed, by trusting that wherever you go you will be of service, you experience tremendous abundance. Like the widow, you discover that there is no end to your supply. Just as your most unique gift to others is being yourself, it is also a gift, which can never be depleted.

Where to Keep Your Focus

You may not be a widow. You may not have debts. You probably don't have creditors threatening to take away your sons as slaves. But the widow's story still applies to you. When your focus is on the things you think you should do, you feel alone, without resources (whether it be physical or financial) and you might feel as if you're a prisoner forced to live the life you don't desire.

Like the widow in the story, you experience freedom and prosperity by focusing on your talents and recognizing how they can benefit others. Reflect for a few minutes today and remember what it is that you truly love about yourself. What do you love to do? Now look for ways to translate that into your business and daily activities. When you pick up your telephone to call your prospects, think only of sharing your oil. You're sure to find empty vessels just waiting to be filled.

I'm not saying that once you focus on your talents, all prospects are suddenly going to want your product or service. But I am saying that once you focus on the gifts that you bring to any interaction, you will notice a difference in your behavior and responses, and that does change the course of your business. I remember seeing that clearly demonstrated a number of years ago by one of the sales associates in my business. She began her sales business part-time, because she was still a full-time employee of another company. She took an instant liking to sales and the immediate success she experienced reflected that. She quickly became one of the top saleswomen in my organization. She even quit smoking and lost 40 pounds within 6 months. Her enthusiasm was perfectly contagious, and her business was showing the fruits of that contagious enthusiasm.

Then one evening she announced to me that she planned to quit the full-time job she hated, so she could devote herself full-time to her sales career. The concern I expressed was that her sales income had not yet completely replaced the income from her full-time job. I suggested she wait just a few more months, until her sales income matched her current income so that she wouldn't feel any unnecessary pressure. She appreciated my advice but decided not to take it.

Within a couple of months I watched as she transformed from being the most positive and influential force at my sales meetings to the most destructive. It was hard to believe she could possibly be the same person. What happened? As soon as she gave up her full-time job, her main source of income had vanished. She obviously needed her sales business to quickly become the significant source of income like her other job had been. Previously she had *enjoyed* sales, but now she *needed* sales.

Once she quit her other job and felt dependent on her sales business, her focus switched from what she could bring to others to what she could get from others through her sales business. Very quickly she faced challenges she had never before experienced — appointments were canceled, new appointments were suddenly hard to get, and the appointments she did have failed to produce the stellar results she'd always experienced. She began to complain about her customers and the company and she even started smoking again. Not long after that, she quit her sales business and went back to her previous profession, probably convinced that this particular company wasn't any good, or that she wasn't cut out for that type of sales business.

I believe she was cut out for sales. I don't think she failed because she wasn't motivated enough or because she had a bad attitude. The negativity she experienced and began to express wasn't the cause of her demise in the company; it was the effect of switching the focus from her desires to her needs. When she began her career, she desired to share with as many people as possible all the benefits of her product and company. When she moved her focus from sharing her product through the expression of her desires to sharing her product because of her needs, the response from her customer base and her potential prospects was completely different.

As long as her focus was on sharing her talents and her product, her sales business was fun and enjoyable, and she attracted a plethora of customers, which is why I believe she was great at sales. However, once she viewed her sales business as her supply and something that she needed, her sales success came to a screeching halt.

Let this story serve you. By keeping your focus on your talents and your desires, which are simply a conglomeration of who you are, you attract plenty of customers. As long as you do that, you won't deplete your ability to continue doing so. However, as soon as you focus on what you need as opposed to what you desire, you fail to authentically express your true essence. Somehow customers and prospects know the difference, and they demonstrate that with their pocketbooks. The sales profession is not a numbers game. The sales profession is a value game. Create value by staying focused on expressing your unique talents. When you do that, you'll have an impressive number of customers and sales.

Lifelong Advice From A
High School English Teacher

When I was a senior in high school, I had the most extraordinary English teacher. His name was Francis Xavier Slevin. He impacted my life so profoundly, that years later I gave our son, Marcus, two middle names, one of which was Xavier, in memory of this teacher who made such a difference in my life. F.X. had reddish brown hair and a very long beard, which he loved to stroke with his fingers. I'll never forget the day he hopped across a fictitious finish line with his spare tire tummy bouncing up and down, to demonstrate and anchor the idea forever in our minds that in life we don't break through a finish line and say, "Ahh! Finally! I've crossed over the finish line. Now, I'm mature."

Have you ever thought that someday you'd break through the finish line and never have to make a tough phone call again? That is only going to happen if you quit working in the sales business. We don't break through the finish line of sales, just as we don't break through the finish line of maturity or knowledge.

Many years ago, one of the saleswomen in my organization had built her business large enough to become a sales manager. I was so impressed with the sales team she had built and I envisioned incredible success for her, until I heard her say, "I can't wait until I'm a manager and I don't have to make anymore of these scary phone calls." I responded by saying, "If you think you're not going to be making anymore scary calls, think again. They're only more intense at the manager level. Instead of calling women to see if they're interested in looking at your product and spending around a hundred dollars, you have to call women you have never met, women who have invested one thousand dollars to sell our product, and they expect you to make them successful."

It was obvious that she didn't believe me. She had mistakenly thought that I had the easy job and she wanted it. Her success as a sales manager was short lived. She thought she had crossed the finish line, when she was promoted to a manager. All that had really happened was that she found herself on a journey in which there was no finish line.

The Song That Never Ends

When my children were young they loved watching a television program call *Lamb Chops*. Shari Lewis, who starred in the show with her adorable puppets, always ended her show with the following lyrics:

> *This is the song that never ends*
> *Oh, it goes on and on my friends.*
> *Some people started singing it, not knowing what it was*
> *and they'll continue singing it forever just because —*

This is the song that never ends
Oh, it goes on and on my friends.
Some people started singing it, not knowing what it was
and they'll continue singing it forever just because —
this is the song that never ends...

If you ever saw that program, you know that Shari would just keep singing and singing that song until the next show started. The song never ended. I'm convinced that Shari was in sales. She must have known that moving from call reluctance to call willingness is a song that never ends, that it goes on and on my friends.

If you've been waiting for the day, when you would finally overcome sales call reluctance or the reluctance to start anything new outside your comfort zone, you've been waiting for a time that will never come. Feeling like you can't do something that you've never done before is a song that never ends. So what if this process is one that never ends? The amazing prize that you experience during this continuous cycle is the opportunity to create value that never ends.

How to Get the Spotlight Off of Fear And On to YOU!

Fear's Favorite Hangout

One of the first things you want to realize is that fear has two favorite hangouts. Do you know where they are? They are the past and the future. Have you ever noticed that? If you're about to make a sales call, fear will rear its ugly head and predict the future and tell you how you'll end up bothering the person, or how you'll end up feeling rejected. Then it will most likely review the past by bringing up past grievances or experiences, which reinforce its position that you are too afraid to make that call.

Fear doesn't talk in terms of the present moment. It only talks about the future and the past. Once you place your focus on the present moment, it's like holding kryptonite up to Superman — fear will shrivel before you.

Why the Mind Dwells on the Past

The mind loves to think about the past because it's a known entity. There are no surprises in it. It's familiar ground and therefore, very comfortable. Whether you think of something that went favorably or unfavorably, you can rev your emotions into high gear by reliving a particular event from your past. Too often we mistake that for true living.

You can think of positive or negative events in your past, but either way, each time you do, you are actually expressing discontent with the present moment. If you're remembering a pleasurable experience, you're being tricked into believing that a previous moment contains more pleasure in it than the present one. When you're recalling an uncomfortable incident, you often find yourself caught up in the fear of repeating the same uncomfortable situation again in some form or another. But ultimately you're being deceived into believing the pain in a previous moment is more intriguing or more powerful than the potential within the present one. The mind dwells on the past, whether it's good or bad, for one reason alone — to avoid the present moment.

How the Mind Steals Your
Future Away From You

If the mind isn't thinking about the past, you can be sure it's focusing on the future. You think about the future usually in two ways, in worry or in aspiration. Have you ever noticed how much you worry about things that never happen? You worry how you'll get everything done before leaving on vacation. You worry how you'll pay all your bills. You worry how a sales prospect will react to you, once you actually make that call. You probably don't believe you want to worry, but the truth is no one is making you do that. You can choose not to worry.

Don't you find relief, when the mind lets go of worry and thinks about the future in a positive way? Do you ever catch yourself dreaming about the way you wish things were? Do you picture what it will be like, after you've done all the things you've been too fearful to do up until now? If so, I have news for you. The false self is up to its usual tricks — it's duping you. You can't live your life in the past or the future. You can only live it now.

Even when you're imagining a bright future, you are actually expressing discontent with the present moment. As long as you express discontent with the present moment, you deny yourself the brighter future you desire because the future is created NOW, in the present. When you express dissatisfaction with the present moment, you are in the process of creating a future in which you'll be dissatisfied. The power to change your future is only in the present moment. As long as you avoid the present moment, whether thinking of the past or thinking of the future, you avoid the power to change.

Fascination with Past and Future Drains Your Current Potential

Have you ever entered a contest in which the winner didn't need to be present to win? Most of us tend to think of that as an advantage. However, my eyes were opened when an acquaintance told me she found the following fortune in a fortune cookie:

Need to be present to win.

The truth in those words is probably more than you imagine. If you're like me, you won't know how little time you spend in the present moment, until you start consciously waking yourself up every chance you can. Understand that studies have shown that people spend over 90% of their time worrying about something that either did or didn't happen in the past or about something that will or won't happen in the future. The only way to stop that is to become aware of the present moment. What facial expression are you making right now? Why? Where are your hands? What's the temperature in the room? If you're tapping your foot, what purpose does it serve?

Becoming consciously aware of the present moment allows one to enjoy the present moment and the splendor there is in it. The power to improve or change yourself or any situation is in the present moment. You can think about tomorrow, but until the morrow arrives, you won't be capable of doing anything to change it.

I remember hearing a talk by Wally Amos in which he said, "Don't blame other people for your dissatisfaction. If you see something you don't like, remember, it starts from within you. You are the single constant in your life." I love that last sentence — you are the single constant in your life. Thus it stands to reason that if something isn't right in your life or it isn't the way you want it, you'll do best by looking within. Even when you deal with other people, you're dealing with them from your own perspective. So in reality, even what you see in others is what you see in yourself. In which case you see yourself everywhere you go (Don't let that scare you!).

The freedom that lies within that concept is that you have the power to make any problem go away, if *you* are the problem! You no longer need to wait for someone to do something, and you no longer need to wait for something to happen. The power to change clearly doesn't lie in the past, and it doesn't even lie in the future, it exists right now in the present moment and in your hands!

You might be thinking, "Oh sure, this all sounds good, but what does it mean?" Let me give you an example. What do you suppose would happen if you caught yourself starting to feel upset and hurt the next time someone said something offensive? Instead of letting the false self jump in, what if you decided to become completely aware of the present moment and then decided not to experience the offense? Can you imagine what it would be like to be free of that emotional roller coaster?

A number of years ago, my husband and I were having lunch out. I was telling him about some things that someone had done (of which I didn't approve), and then I said, "Can you believe she's done all that, after I've been such a good manager to her?" He bravely said to me, "I don't know that I'd say you've been a good manager to her. You've been a good support to her."

In that instant I was able to catch myself feeling enraged by his comment and in that very present moment instead of letting anger take over, I decided to be silent and deliberately not take offense to his comment. Within seconds I had a tremendous sense of relief and guess what else happened? I realized he was not trying to offend me at all; he was providing powerful insight into a frustrating situation. This woman was taking advantage of me in ways she wouldn't have, if I'd been less of a support system to her and more of a manager. That insight allowed me to understand how I could dramatically improve my business relationships with the women in my sales unit. In addition, I prevented a ridiculous argument between my husband and me.

If I had not become aware of the present moment and what I was feeling, I can assure you that the false self was prepared to instantly take over, and I would have found myself recalling all similar past grievances between my husband and me. By waking up to the present moment and refusing to take offense, I opened the door to unexpected grace, and my husband and I shared a wonderfully memorable lunch together. In fact, I still remember what we ate for lunch that day and how much fun we had.

Waking yourself up to the present moment can also greatly assist you with a very popular sales topic — overcoming rejection. Let's face it, no matter how fantastic your opening script is or even how smoothly you handle objections, everyone will not always say yes to you, your product or your service. I don't believe the secret is to simply "Get over it," and forge ahead. A few years ago, I heard about a woman who made 100 prospecting calls a day and was very successful but who simultaneously felt deeply dissatisfied. When asked how she could envision her business becoming what she wanted, she simply replied, "I make 100 prospecting calls a day." She had taught herself how to forge ahead, but she'd obviously lost a sense of connectedness with her business and her clients. She'd become like a robot; she made her 100 calls every day, and every day she made her 100 calls. But where is the value in that? Nowhere. Her business was unpalatable to her because it completely lacked value.

We often entertain the idea that the sales business is all about numbers. However, when your sales business actually becomes all about numbers, it loses purpose and therefore value. The way to forge ahead without losing your purpose, your "oil," is to consciously decide not to take offense and not to feel rejected, right in that very moment of being rejected. The difficulty in that stems from the old adage that there are two sides to every story. We mistakenly believe that those two sides are things like "my way or not my way," "I'm right or I'm wrong," or "I'm rejected or I'm not rejected." In other words, the two sides of the story are winning and losing. Actually, that's just one side of the story, namely, the win/lose side. The other side of the story is win/win. When I decided not to take offense in the comment my husband made about me not being a good manager to the one sales representative, we automatically moved to the side of win/win. I learned a valuable lesson in how to work more effectively with individuals who were also good friends and I was able to recognize how honest my husband was willing to be with me, which strengthened my trust in him.

When you decide not to feel rejected because a prospect

declines your product or service, you'll automatically move to the win/win side as well. It isn't necessary to review your past and study why you're so petrified of rejection. You can't change the past. You can only change the present moment. The next time you start to feel rejected by a prospect or a customer, step into the present moment, the side of win/win, and simply decide not to take offense. Who knows the value you'll find there? Maybe you'll suddenly grasp why a certain technique or manner you've used is ineffective, or maybe you'll finally see things from your prospect's point of view, which will only improve your ability to sell to your next prospect. The one thing that's definite is that you and that prospect are sure to experience value. Every time you focus on the value you create, it brings you back to the present moment.

If your focus is on the present moment, the opportunity there is immeasurable. When you become aware and grateful of the blessings right now, your past disappears and your future reflects the joy and abundance that's become your focus. Staying in the present moment is a secret weapon over which fear and the false self have no power.

There's no need for you to wish things worked out differently in the past or to wish that things could be like they used to be. There's no need for you to anxiously hope that things will be better in the future, or to dread the worst possible scenario. Every time you do that, you're robbing yourself of the joy to be found in today. Indeed, the only moment you have is right now and right now and right now. The only chance you have to change yourself is right now and right now. Change can only be found in the present moment — not in the past and not in the future — just right now. The next time you hear of a contest, in which the winner need not be present to win, become aware of the present moment and know that true fortunes come from being present.

Is Fear Really Real?

Many of us are familiar with Franklin Roosevelt's words, "The only thing to fear is fear itself." In actuality, however, we don't even need to bother with fearing fear. Martin Luther King Jr. implied that fear isn't even real with his words, "Fear knocked at the door. Faith answered. No one was there." The question I used to ask myself was "How can something that feels so real not be?"

Most people consider reality to be the things that they identify by using their five senses. If, for example, you saw a sewing machine, it's highly probable you'd say it's real because you could see it and feel it. Naturally we tend to believe that reality is comprised of those things we see, feel, hear, taste and/or smell. But what if I were to set fire to that visible, tangible sewing machine and I were to burn it until nothing visible or tangible remained? Would the reality of the sewing machine be destroyed?

Think of the qualities expressed by the sewing machine — usefulness, creativity, expediency — these qualities represented by the sewing machine remain forever intact. No fire can ever touch them. And because those qualities remain forever intact, they are the only reality the sewing machine ever possessed. In other words, reality isn't physical. The physical object we see is the manifestation of reality, but in and of itself, it isn't reality. You can destroy every sewing machine in the world, but you can't take away the idea of a sewing machine. The idea behind any one thing contains the enduring qualities of that thing, which constitute its *true reality*.

My friend and mentor, Miss Freda Dixon, just about saw the entire last century. She passed on just a few months before her 100th birthday. But her leaving this world could never take Freda away from me. She lives forever in my thoughts. Her magnificent qualities remain forever intact.   It isn't her body that constituted her reality, but rather the enduring qualities expressed by this dear amazing woman.

Maybe you've felt fear. Perhaps you've even seen its effect. But it only *feels* real because you believe it is. The only identity it can ever have is the identity *you give it.*   Freda once told me, "For years they thought the world was flat. Did that keep it from being round?" For years people thought the world was flat. Did that keep it from being round? The belief that the world was flat was the perceived identity, but that belief had no place in reality.

Our world has never been flat. The limitation was due to the belief not to the world. Likewise, it is the belief in fear that produces limitations. You have no real limitations.

If you're thinking of ways to conquer fear, you must stop. Thinking that fear needs to be conquered is partnered by thinking it is real. Once you act as though it is real, limitations appear. Only by walking through fear, by doing what you are afraid to do, will you behold the nothingness of it. It's just a big fat zero! You think you feel it and see it, but in truth it has no enduring qualities.   With no true reality of its own, fear can never really touch who you truly are.

What's Behind the Curtain?

I am of the opinion that The Wizard of Oz is one of the greatest movies ever produced in Hollywood. All of the main characters in the story go on the perilous search to meet the supposed all-powerful Wizard of Oz, in the hope that he can give them what they are certain they lack. Dorothy wants to get back home, the Scarecrow desires a brain, the Tin Man yearns for a heart, and the Lion seeks courage.

Throughout their journey they have several encounters with a frightening wicked witch, who continually suggests that they'll never find what they're seeking because she has the power to stop them. She uses different tactics to scare them away, but no matter how frightened they are of her, they just keep moving along the yellow brick road to reach their destination – the Emerald City, where the Wizard of Oz resides.

When they reach the palace of the Wizard of Oz, they discover, much to their chagrin, that the wizard isn't a friendly guy, who happily grants wishes to the people who face the perilous journey to find him. Instead, the wizard is a huge, fantastical head on a throne, with a stern and loud, powerful voice. And he doesn't grant them their wishes; in fact, he refuses to assist them unless they defeat the wicked witch and bring him her broomstick.

Although feeling certain that each of them is no match for their greatest foe, they vow to try their best. Finally, after a long and stressful journey, they are all in the witch's castle trying desperately to run away from her, but end up being cornered by her and all her evil demons. Without even consciously planning it, they take a stand against her and witness that she melts before their eyes. Suddenly all the demons pay homage to our heroes and gladly give them the witch's broomstick, which they promptly take to the great Wizard of Oz.

When our heroes return with the requested broom in order to receive their desires, the Wizard of Oz denies them their requests and says, "Come back tomorrow." Even though they are trembling and shaking, they stay put and persist to ask for what they want. Then they notice something moving behind a curtain. When they pull back the curtain, a little old man stands in front of a board of electrical machinery. The facade ends, as they realize the supposedly all-powerful Wizard of Oz is no more than a timid little man, who's been hiding behind a curtain.

Our heroes demand to collect the things they were told the Wizard could give them — a brain for the Scarecrow, a heart for the Tin Man, courage for the Lion, and a trip back home for Dorothy. But the supposedly great and all-powerful Wizard of Oz can't grant them their requests. And why? Because he can't give them what they already possess or have the ability to manifest on their own.

The journey of these four characters parallels your journey in overcoming the self-sabotage of phone anxiety or any other self-defeating habits. You have dreams and goals of what it will feel like to be successful. You dream of having what it takes to achieve that success. But before long you encounter those wicked trouble thoughts that tell you how scared and fearful you feel in the pursuit your dreams. Still unwilling to give up, you hope that someone somewhere will say or do something that has a wizard-like effect on you, so you no longer feel afraid.

Sometimes you even see or experience a wizard like display of motivation, but you leave only to discover that you're still trapped in the castle of fear. Then, just as everything seems hopeless, you dare to take a step you were too afraid to take. As you walk up to face your greatest fear, it melts before your eyes. Reflecting on all it required to bring you to this point, you learn that you always had the ability to do what you were sure you couldn't; you just didn't realize it until now. You've always had security, intelligence, love and courage, but you've been looking for it outside of yourself. You must look within to discover all the qualities you wish to express or to be expressed in your life.

How to Turn Fear into a Friend

Just like our heroes in the Wizard of Oz, you want to avoid the wicked witch of fear at all times. But remember how the witch melted before them, as soon as they faced her? Once they witnessed the nothingness of fear, they gained a sense of courage they thought they lacked. Indeed, they gathered enough courage to face the next fear. Once they dared to face that fear, they learned their fear had only been a wizard's illusion. Each time they faced their fears, they peeled off a layer of self-doubt and unveiled a new level of self-esteem.

You are the hero in your life. Each time you face fear, you too watch in childish excitement as it dissipates before you. You want to believe that you'll conquer it for good. But fear refuses to admit defeat, and before you realize it, you find yourself once again in the back seat of the car with that evil twin in the front seat at the wheel. Over and over you have to move to the front and face your fear. Over and over you watch fear dissipate before your eyes, while the beauty of your dreams unfolds.

You can't run away from your fears any more than you can run away from your own shadow. Just as you would never mistake your shadow for the real you, never mistake fear as a real part of you. Learn its routine and know that as soon as you begin to see even a hint of the shadow of fear, you must be on the right path.

Fear never bothers to present itself when you're not working toward a dream or goal. It seems to be your foe, because you think it's stopping you from taking the needed steps that move you toward your desires. But fear's power disappears as quickly as you begin to do what it tells you you're too afraid to do. Let fear show you that you must really want to take the next step — if you didn't, there would be no fear around it. Begin to embrace the fear you feel; see it as a wonderful guide, always clearly pointing in the direction you want to move. Walk up to it, welcome it in your life, and know that as you take the next step holding its hand, you are walking on the path of self-fulfillment.

Why You Don't Have To <u>Feel</u> Successful To <u>Be</u> Successful

The Challenge in Feeling Successful

Have you ever noticed how quickly you can lose the confidence to make a call or contact a prospect because you don't feel like you can do it? The reasons why you don't feel you can do something as simple as making a phone call are varied. You might feel it's because you lack experience, confidence, or previous success.

The problem is that you've probably heard that you need to feel like you can do something before you can, or that you need to feel like you can succeed at something before you can. Therefore, you can achieve anything, if you can *feel* like you're achieving it. Well, I say, "NO!" You can't take your feelings to the bank. Furthermore, you don't have to feel successful at first to end up being successful.

The Best Way to Feel Successful

One of the most powerful tips that I've stated in different ways throughout this book is that the very things we think we need before we take action, like courage, confidence and comfort, are the things that only come to us *after we've taken action.* Likewise, the only way to truly *feel* successful is to take action.

You can't sit around waiting or hoping to some day *feel* successful. Only by taking action, even when you don't feel successful at the moment, do you discover how to feel successful. Whenever you wait to take action, you defer feeling successful.

There's no need to think that something is wrong with you and that you need to wait until you feel successful. Grasp that you don't have to feel successful to be successful. You don't need to wait until you feel successful because you're never going to feel like you are successful until you've done the task ahead of you. If the feelings of success are only generated through activity, it just doesn't make sense to wait until you feel successful before acting.

Think of all the times you've waited to do something that you want or need to do. Any time you see yourself waiting, you can remember that you're waiting for naught. If you've thought about doing something, if you've thought about calling a prospect, you must want to do it NOW! That's why you think about it. You don't think about it so you can put it on a list to do later, when you have the courage to do it. You think of it because it's something you want to do now. When you get in the habit of doing the things you're sure you don't feel successful enough to do, you can take results to the bank!

Was Napoleon Hill Wrong?

You've probably heard of Napoleon Hill's book, *Think and Grow Rich*. Hill's premise in that book is the same as his famous quote, "Whatever the mind can conceive and believe, the body can achieve." Hill highly suggests that you write down a description of your chief aim in life and that you repeat it to yourself while looking in the mirror, every morning upon waking and every evening before retiring. I wouldn't be a bit surprised if many people, who suggest that you have to feel successful before you can be successful, have read Napoleon Hill's books.

Am I saying that he was wrong? No, I'm not. Look at Hills' famous quote and the basic premise of all his writings, "Whatever the mind can conceive and believe, the body can achieve." Notice that Hill doesn't say, "After the mind conceives of something, put the idea on a "to do" list, wait around until you feel successful, and then you can achieve it."

Napoleon Hill himself was a man of action and he made decisions quickly. When he was asked by Andrew Carnegie if he was willing to devote 20 years of his life (during which time he was to make his own living) to meeting and interviewing the 500 most successful men in the nation at that time in order to discover the habits of successful people, Hill required only 29 seconds before blurting out, "Yes." He tells this story in his book (and my personal favorite), *Grow Rich with Peace of Mind*. In that book he also reveals that in those 29 seconds he met with the trouble thoughts that cajoled him and tried to convince him that he didn't have what it would take to achieve it.

If Napoleon Hill had waited around to feel like he was successful, he would never have been able to make that decision to say, "Yes" in 29 seconds. He recounts that he found his positive attitude in those seconds. The positive attitude that says, "Yes, I'm willing to take a risk and do what I may not feel successful enough to do right now, but deep inside I know that I can achieve this, if I just get started now!"

It comes down to this, if you want to move in the direction of your dreams and desires, you must develop a habit of taking an important step toward that desire daily. Typically the important things that move you in the direction of obtaining your desires are not routine. You probably won't see yourself as "having the time" to do them. You probably won't see yourself as "having the courage" to do them either. However, you very quickly manifest your dreams when you decide rapidly (29 seconds is good) to do what's important, no matter what the trouble thoughts are saying to you about time or courage.

Is Doing More Powerful Than Thinking?

I definitely believe in the power of thought. I've seen in my own life how different experiences and situations are a result of what I was thinking at that time. However, just sitting on my couch all day and thinking won't profit me much, if I never take any form of action. Before I met my husband, I envisioned the type of relationship I desired with a partner, which I believe proved beneficial. However, I believe the chances are slim that my dream partner would have knocked on my door, if I had spent hours a day thinking of the perfect relationship, but had never left my house.

Be careful not to use thinking as a means to cop-out of doing. That is the danger in listening to a trouble thought that says you don't *feel* successful enough to take action. If you stop yourself from taking action on an important goal in order to get yourself feeling positive, all you've really done is stop yourself from taking action. Every time you let those trouble thoughts talk you out of taking action, you continually augment the difficulty of taking action. The false self loves to talk you out of moving forward and then chastise you for not doing so.

One of the best ways to stop that insanity is to take action. Action isn't more valuable than thought. Thought isn't more valuable than action. However, by combining both of them you definitely create what Buckminster Fuller coined as "synergy." Synergy is the interaction of two forces in a manner that their combined effect is greater than the sum of their individual effects. The key is to observe the patterns in your life that have ultimately created what you've been getting, and thereby learn how you can combine the forces of thought and action to get what you desire.

A Trip 8,000 Feet "Down Under"

A number of years ago I was given a very rare opportunity. I was heading out to Lead, South Dakota, to do some sales training for Donna Job, a leader in my sales organization. Her husband, Steve, was the superintendent of the gold mine in Lead, and he offered to take me on a tour of the mine. Naturally I accepted the offer.

At a sales conference, a few weeks before I went to South Dakota, I ran into a gentleman friend and told him of the adventure ahead of me. When I bragged that I'd be going 8,000 feet underground, he laughed heartily at me. I remember him saying, "Tammy, I'll have to teach you about decimal points and how they can change the number of zeros after a number." Doubting my intelligence, I said, "Oh. Maybe it's just 800 feet." He said, "I'm sure it is." Just then (no kidding) my friend Donna walked by. I stopped her and said, "Tell this guy about the trip we're going to make down to the gold mine." She then proceeded to explain that we'd be traveling 8,000 feet underground. The look on this man's face was priceless. He started to say, "But that's..." Donna replied, "Half way to China." Then he said, "It must be hotter than..." Donna said, "Hell. Yes, it is." That was certainly a moment in which I felt I couldn't design my life more perfectly!

I didn't realize the opportunity that truly awaited me, until I arrived at the mine. This mine was not open to the public. Even the employees of the mine could only take one person on a tour each year. Currently the mine is completely closed. Perhaps some day it will be turned into a tourist facility, but at that time and even while I write this book, the opportunity afforded me was very rare indeed.

Before going down the mine, I actually had to sign a legal document agreeing that I would take no legal action and that my family would take no legal action, if anything happened to me or if I was killed. We've all heard the expression, "to sign one's life away." I actually *experienced* that expression. I was given a special suit to put on, as well as a hard hat and special glasses, and then I entered a shaft that dropped 8,000 feet underground. At some point in my adult life, I was no longer able to handle the rides at the state fair; maybe it was after that event. I had soared above the ground plenty of times in an airplane, but I'd never dropped below the earth's surface.

The Amazing Qualities of Gold

The day "down under" with Donna and Steve impressed me tremendously.   It was a whole city underground, except that instead of buildings there was huge mining machinery. I could hardly accept the picture before my eyes. Then I learned some remarkable statistics.

Did you know that gold is one of the heaviest chemical elements? It's nineteen times as heavy as water, yet at the same time it's one of the most easily worked metals. Indeed just one tiny gram can be shaped and hammered to form a wire a mile long. If that isn't mind boggling enough, the miners in Lead, South Dakota, mined one ton of rock for a piece of gold the size of a chocolate chip. So valuable is gold!

The Refining Process

The amazing underground city I explored that day owed its excavation to the value of gold. Yet, whether found in nature as dust or as nuggets, gold is seldom pure. A very necessary process, in order to obtain the value is refining. Look at that one more time. A very necessary process in order to obtain value is refining.

During the refining process of gold, the dross is separated from the gold. The dictionary defines dross as "scum that rises to the top of molten metal." Yes. That's right, S-C-U-M. That worthless refuse, that foamy vile, despicable stuff. Scum.

Separate the Dross from Your Gold

After my trip into the gold mine, I realized that quite similar to gold, moving from call reluctance to call willingness had within it the opportunity of refinement as well. I suggest you start thinking of those trouble thoughts that you hear before picking up the telephone or before attempting anything outside your comfort zone as "the dross." The trouble thoughts that keep you from your goals all day long and then chastise you before you go to bed because you didn't reach your goals — hey, if that isn't scum, I don't know what is.

Just as you seldom find pure gold, you seldom have a day devoid of that false self. You needn't set unreal expectations for yourself. You simply accept the process of refining. Just as the beauty and powerful qualities of gold seem hidden until it is separated from the dross, you can never know your own capabilities until you separate yourself from the false self. Just as dross has no value, there's no reason to value and heed the advice of those nagging, scummy, trouble thoughts.

You Have No Competition

One of the most fascinating interviews I ever listened to was one with Dr. Lawrence Doyle, who is a principal investigator with S.E.T.I. Institute at the NASA Ames Research Center. In the interview he explained that according to some calculations there are some 5 billion people on this little water covered planet, and if all those people were to jump into the ocean at once, the ocean would raise only one tenth of an inch. One million of our earths could be dropped inside the sun, and one million suns would fit in some of the other stars in the galaxy. When one understands the size of the known universe, one could say that materially speaking, each of us is completely insignificant.

But Dr Doyle maintained that no person is negligible for the following reason. If you found a piece of gold, and if it were the only gold to be found in that mine in Lead, South Dakota, it would definitely be extremely valuable. However, if it were the only gold to be found in the entire nation, it would be worth a great deal more. If this gold you found were the only gold in existence, it would be irreplaceable.

So what is your gold? It is that with which no one else can compete. I will never forget hearing Dr Doyle ask, "Who can compete with you at being yourself?" Those words are so freeing. Your greatest gift to others is being yourself, and what a rare gift that is. It is in being yourself that you have absolutely no competition. If you consider that most business owners would give anything to eliminate the competition, your marketing position, when it comes to being yourself, is priceless. This is something to remember before picking up your telephone or during any action you take in your business. The most unique feature you bring to your business is you, it's irreplaceable and beyond any monetary value.

Certainly one of the things those trouble thoughts love to

forecast is all the competition you'll face. How often they scare you out of action, just because someone else is doing better! However, by continually reminding yourself to focus on your expression of your gifts and talents, you can stay on a positive course of action, as opposed to inaction. The competition you face in a sales business becomes less and less significant, as you realize how little competition you actually have.

When our son, Marcus, was a little boy, he asked my husband and me how much we thought the Mona Lisa painting was worth. I answered that we couldn't say because it was considered priceless. Then Marcus said, "Oh yeah, I know that. But how much would it cost, if you wanted to buy it." My husband then explained that the painting was in the Louvre museum and wasn't for sale because the museum didn't want to sell it. Still Marcus persisted with, "Oh, I know that. But if they were going to sell it, how much do you think they'd sell it for?" We tried to firm up our voices by saying, "Son, they wouldn't sell it because it's priceless to them. No amount of money can justify selling it." What do you think he said? "I know, I know. But how much do you think it would sell for, if they did decide to sell it?"

I believe the reason Marcus was so persistent was due to his perception that all material items must ultimately have a price. Although the original Mona Lisa is unique, most of us wouldn't know if we were looking at the original or just a copy. The screenplay of the movie, The Thomas Crown Affair, deals with that precise subject. If a museum, like the Louvre, decided that only copies of paintings would be represented, how much would people pay to own the originals? Perhaps our son had a point – ultimately those paintings would sell for a price.

However, no one can ever make a copy of you. Even a clone of you would fail to be like you because it wouldn't have the same experiences and thoughts and emotions that you've had all your life. It truly is impossible to place a monetary value on a human life because we seldom understand how much we can affect other people's lives.

The Perfection in Rarity

It never ceases to amaze me how unique we all are from one another. My husband and I have four children and we are continually intrigued by their individuality. We can talk for hours about each of them and still never come close to truly understanding what it's like to be any of them.

The fact that there is no one at all exactly like you, demonstrates the perfection of the universe to continually express infinity as personal individuality. Just as a jeweler describes the qualities that constitute a perfect diamond, the qualities that constitute your description make you perfect. You embody perfection because you are the only one capable of being you.

Carpe Phonum

To all you sales people out there, I say, "CARPE PHONUM." Seize the telephone and discover gold — the gold of being yourself. No one can compete with you at being authentically you. It cannot be denied that you are irreplaceable. Embrace this truth and enjoy the expression of you and your uniqueness in your life and in your business.

Dialing a prospect's phone number is the refining process, which separates your gold from the worthless trouble thoughts that would contaminate you. You may have to go deep past the initial trouble voices to discover this gold. Its weight is heavy; more worth is there than you ever expected. But once discovered, it is so easy to shape and hammer out a life of pure joy that goes on and on and on.

Embrace Your Greatness

Of course, we've all heard many times over that there's no one else like us. But we often use that incredible fact to stop us from enjoying our present state or taking action toward something we desire. We look at others, whom we view as more successful, and see that they have something we lack. Fortunately simple stories often unveil convoluted truths. Look at all the golden nuggets in this simple little story of the three caterpillars. One day as three caterpillars are busy eating, a butterfly soars above them. The first little caterpillar shouts, "Oh, look at that butterfly showing off!" The second little caterpillar cries out, "Oh, I wish I could be like her." But the third little caterpillar brilliantly exclaims, "That's me!"

That's such a simple little story, but look at the implicit truths within it. Considering that all the caterpillars will soon be butterflies, the first little caterpillar's scornful remark is unwarranted, and the second caterpillar has no reason to feel envious. But how true that it certainly stings, when we see others excelling, if we don't recognize our capability to excel at being ourselves is no less than anyone else's. Few things are more ascetic than condemning that which we secretly desire to become. And how dangerous it is to fall into the trap of believing that what is possible for others simply can't be for us. The freedom in rising above mediocrity and fully expressing ourselves is a *process*, much like the metamorphosis of a caterpillar into a butterfly.

Where the signs of self-sabotage are blatant in the comments of the first and the second caterpillar, the jubilant voice of self-actualization is expressed by the third. The third caterpillar is wise enough to see herself capable of her desires. She displays no judgment or agitation with the progress of another, but is only inspired by it. The third caterpillar doesn't resent the butterfly that has what she wants; she rejoices in its manifestation of her goals and dreams.

Isn't it interesting that the caterpillars that display the most resistance are unhappy with their current situation and the present moment, while the one who identifies with her present surroundings easily expresses joy and enthusiasm? There's no magic pill that transforms us into our desired state overnight. However, if we trust and know that life is a process, the changes we yearn for occur rather quickly.

What Keeps Us Forever From Learning

Bernard Shaw said, "If you teach a man anything, he will never learn. It is in doing that he learns." You can read hundreds of books on the subject of overcoming fear, you can listen to hundreds of motivational speakers on the subject of how to get motivated, but you will continue to wait on your dreams and desires. Only if while trembling and shaking you take the step that you're afraid to take, will you learn. It is in dialing the prospect's phone number and then speaking with that prospect that you learn just how capable you are of doing something before you have the courage to do so. What keeps you forever from learning is the resistance to put yourself in the game. As long as you wait along the sidelines to gather up the confidence you need, you'll never feel confident enough to do anything but hang out along the sidelines.

No matter how great your sales success was yesterday, today is always the beginning of a clean slate. Without the courage to do so, you have to rise out of the dugout of fear and put yourself back in the game. That is definitely a song that never ends. Each time that you rise up, take a step in a direction you've never gone before, knowing that courage will only accompany you after you've taken action, you create value in your life and in other people's lives. The more value you create, the more you will see continued good unfold in your life. Gratefulness for that good is next to godliness. And remember, the highest form of gratitude in the last couple of millenniums and in the next has been and always will be action. Take action! Don't wait!

Get What You Want

The Way Out of a Dungeon

There's an old tale about a man who was taken prisoner many years ago somewhere in not so distant land. He was dragged down a long flight of stairs, thrown into a dungeon, and the prison door was slammed shut. For twenty years he lived in darkness, alone and miserable. Finally one day he decided that he couldn't stand this form of existence any longer. He would rather die than continue to live in such a manner. He then devised a plan to attack the guard, who brought him his food each morning. He reasoned that he would be killed and put out of his misery, once he attempted to attack the guard.

In order to prepare himself for his attack, he decided to become more familiar with his prison cell. As it was completely dark, he groped along the walls in order to situate himself near the door. When he found the prison door, to his surprise, it was unlocked and could easily be pushed open.

Slowly with his now weak limbs, he ascended the long flight of stairs. When he spotted two prison guards at the top of the stairs, he knew he had little time left to live. But as he drew near, the guards stepped aside and let him pass. As he made his way out of the prison, each guard he saw stepped aside for him. Finally he walked out of the prison, into a gorgeous green meadow, a free man.

This story is every man's story. How long will you listen to the voice whose only goal is to keep you in the dark, feeling imprisoned with no way out? How long before you take the step to walk away from a snickering voice that threatens you can't? How long before you rise up against it, only to find that it never had any real hold on you, no power and no worth.

Each day that we continue to mindlessly obey the nagging trouble thoughts can be compared to each day the man in our story spent in a dark and cold prison. The day we begin to learn to ignore those trouble thoughts is likewise the day of our liberation. There are times we may find ourselves back in that dark dungeon cell, but it doesn't take long for us wake up out of that dreary state to remember that the prison door is open, and that we never need feel imprisoned by any thought or situation.

The first step toward progress is willingness, willingness to be brutally honest with oneself about oneself. Here's a reason to get started with that process: as soon as you desire to become aware of whom you really are, you are aware. Awareness is a great place to be. Think about that. From the point of awareness you are no longer in the dark, mindlessly obeying the trouble thoughts that would lead you astray all day long every day for the rest of your life. Couple willingness with awareness and you can change anything in your life.

Willingness to be aware of the false self reveals what a deceiver it is. Begin to realize how it has taken control in areas you never imagined. Expose its counterproductive solutions and watch it melt and wither away. The key to ending any undesired behavior isn't the understanding that you no longer desire that behavior. The key to eliminating undesired habits is doing the opposite of what that false voice says. Dare to walk right past its prison guards to discover there are no guards and there is no prison.

Watch Out For Your Beliefs

In the preceding story, the man's belief that he is imprisoned is what actually keeps him imprisoned. When he finally entertains taking some kind of action to escape his imprisoned condition, he learns that nothing ever prevented him from a life of freedom other than his own belief system. It seems crazy that someone could be trapped in a dark prison for years and years without knowing that the doors to the prison are unlocked, until we uncover the transparent beliefs that often keep us locked up, living a life far from our liking. Like the man in the story, those beliefs keep us in a seeming prison, until we, on our own accord, break free.

I'll share a very personal story to illustrate that. When I was two years old, my father was killed in an airplane crash. I had one sibling, my older brother, Jim, who was five. Our mother was only 26 at the time. It was devastating. Naturally, I developed certain beliefs from that painful event and the dysfunctional family dynamics that ensued.

During my years of growing up, I didn't consciously know the conclusions I'd made from the trauma I experienced as a toddler. I only knew that I was always going way out of my way to make things nice for others. I often did tasks only to make people happy.

Years later, as an adult with a family and a business of my own, I began to explode over issues that really had very little to do with me. As much as I tried, I couldn't seem to figure out why I was feeling such intense anxiety. One day I decided to just stop trying to figure it out. I even said to the Universe, "I don't know anymore. You show me."

Just a few days after that voiced request, a dear friend of mine and I had the opportunity to be together and take a long three-hour walk in downtown Dallas. That night, I opened up to her about all the things I was going through. By the end of the night we could both see it all so clearly. In order to survive a terrible tragedy and to create a sense of purpose, I had developed a belief that I must do whatever I could to maintain the happiness and/or status quo around me. It was as if I wore a little sign around my neck that said, "Little Miss Fix-It." As long as I carried that little sign along as part of my belief system, everyone responded to it by expecting me to help solve their problems and letting me. As a child without her daddy, this belief seemed to serve me well because it made me feel that I could control the happiness around me. But as an adult, it was making me crazy! Feeling like it was up to me to go around and try to solve people's problems was a transparent belief. In other words, it was ruling me but I didn't know it because I couldn't even see it.

My personal beliefs had definitely evolved since I was a young girl. As an adult, I had come to believe that each person is responsible for her/his own life. But the belief that I had to be "Little Miss Fix-It" was still running the show. All the situations that frustrated me did so because I felt like I had to fix them. And ultimately, I resented feeling like I had to fix everything. The turmoil I experienced inside was due to a major conflict of beliefs — one that said people are responsible for their own lives and the other that said you have to go fix everyone's life and make it better. Like the man in the dungeon, I was completely imprisoned by the belief that told me it was up to me to keep others happy. When I reached the point where I couldn't stand to be in that prison any longer, it was revealed that the only one keeping me locked inside was me.

Hopefully that story demonstrates the importance in watching out for your beliefs. Some of the beliefs, that are directing the course of your life by determining the people and the events that come into your experience, can actually be undermining what you deeply desire.

I can't stress enough how powerful it is to release limited binding beliefs. As the desire to rid yourself of all limiting beliefs increases, you simultaneously increase your awareness of the destructive beliefs that you mentally express, in addition to the destructive beliefs that you verbally express. Once you become conscious of the negative talk going on inside your head, you can join the present moment and start to reprogram what you think and say.

Those Tricky Don't Wants

Have you ever ended up with something you didn't want in your life? Maybe the job you have isn't the job you actually want. Maybe the sales force you lead doesn't perform at the level you desire. Maybe your family members don't do the things you wish they would. When things like that happen, you tend to think it's out of your control. If you were in control, it would all be different. Your life would be the way you want it.

What if all those things were actually in your control? Picture this:

You're in a restaurant and a waiter comes up and asks you what you want. You begin by saying, "Wow, that forest mushroom soup sure sounds good, but I don't know if I just want soup. Can you tell me if the tuna is fresh? Wait! Never mind about that. I've heard it has too much mercury. You know, the Caesar salad is tempting, but I just don't know if that will fill me up."

Tell me, what's the waiter going to do for you at this point? Maybe the better question is this, what can the waiter do for you? Obviously nothing because you haven't even decided what you want.

In that example lies one of the secrets to getting what you want from all those prospecting calls you make. You have to decide and know what it is that you want. Do you know what you want from your prospecting calls? You're probably thinking, "Are you nuts? Of course, I know what I want. I want to generate sales."

I believe you. That is, I believe you believe that. You see, my experience tells me that you wouldn't be reading this book right now, if you were already getting exactly what you want from all your prospecting calls. Let me show you what I think is really going on. Before I can do that, however, I need you to read the following short paragraph and pay attention to how many times I use my phrase, "Carpe Phonum."

It was my business coach who first gave me the idea to write a program called "Call Reluctance Reversed." I loved the idea and acted quickly on it. Because I used the phrase, "seize the phone," in the speech, a friend of mine couldn't help but think of the Latin phrase, "Carpe Diem – Seize the Day." That's the story of how "Call Reluctance Reversed" became "Carpe Phonum – Seize the Phone."

NOW, without looking back on that paragraph, can you tell me how many times I used a word that started with the letter "b"? Most likely not. And why should you be able to, right? You were looking for the phrase, "Carpe Phonum."

Here's my point: You know how many times I used the phrase "Carpe Phonum" because that's what you were focused on. No big surprise there, right? But more times than you can possibly believe right now, you are not focused on what you want, and that's truly why you don't get it.

When most sales professionals are about to pick up that phone, they aren't just thinking about getting a sale. They're hoping their prospect won't be rude. They're hoping their prospect won't raise an objection that they fail to handle.

They're hoping they don't get voice mail again. They're hoping they won't sound nervous, etc.

Do you relate to any of that? If so, then notice that some of those things that you "want" are actually things that you don't want. How are you supposed to get what you want while thinking about what you don't want? Remember how easy it was to see how many times I used the phrase "Carpe Phonum"? It was easy because you're mind was predominantly focused on one thing. However, what if I had asked you to pay attention to how many words I wrote that started with the letter "t" and how many times I used the word "reluctance," and how many times I didn't use a word that ended with a "d"? That would have been a bit much to stay focused on and achieve the right answer.

Likewise, it's a bit much to achieve what you want from prospecting, when you have so many things going through your mind, as to what you want, what you don't want, what you can't forget, what you must remember to say, etc. Before I make my calls, I just take a deep breath and focus on one thing – create value. That's my goal. Just to create value. Maybe I'll do it by being a friendly voice to the executive assistant. Maybe I'll do it by having the product or service my prospect is looking for. Maybe I won't be able to create value. But, I stop all that nonsense going on in my head that just scares me out of making the calls I need and want to make. By staying focused on one thing – I often get it.

Look at all the thoughts going on in your head today before you make your prospecting calls. Would getting focused on one thing assist you to seize that telephone?

How The Language of "Don't Want" Creates Unwanted Results

Did you ever notice that most people actually talk about what they want by describing what they don't want? Look at some of these examples:

> *"I don't want to pay such high taxes."*
>
> *"I don't want to end up with nothing after*
>   *paying my bills."*
>
> *"I don't want to gain back the weight I've lost."*
>
> *"I don't want to get divorced like so many others."*
>
> *"I don't want to get sick and die young like my parents."*
>
> *"I don't want to get fired from my job."*
>
> *"I don't want to be single the rest of my life."*
>
> *"I don't want to drive in traffic everyday."*
>
> *"I don't want to come home to a dirty house."*
>
> *"I don't want to have to work the rest of my life."*
>
> *"I don't want to feel like a failure."*
>
> *"I don't want to live like this."*

Perhaps you have said or thought things similar to those phrases above. I challenge you today to pay attention to your words and how you describe what it is that you want. Becoming clear about what you *do* want doesn't involve describing what you *don't* want. This means that all comparison factors must be left unattended. You are not focusing on what you want, when you're comparing it to something that you don't want.

As an example, you don't attract the habit of keeping a clean office by saying, "I've got to stop keeping such a messy office." That thought actually continues to attract the habits that keep you from producing what it is you actually desire. You block out the ideas you would generate as to how to keep a clean office by continually repeating that your office is messy. However, by focusing on your desire to keep a well organized office that allows you to easily find what you need, you'll find yourself thinking of ideas that align with that desire and taking action steps that coincide as well.

Why We Continue To Get What We Don't Want

I'll share with you the story of the white tile in our house in Arizona because it shows the power of focusing on what you don't want and the power of focusing on what you do want.

When Jim and I moved to Arizona in 1999, we needed to find a house rather quickly, as our furniture was due to arrive within a couple of weeks. We really wanted to live in the city of Tempe, but there were not many homes available for sale at that time. We finally found a house with a floor plan that would work for our fairly large family. The floor plan was fine, but I never could tolerate the appearance of the house. Throughout the entry way and the kitchen there was this small white tile that was impossible to keep clean. For three years I thought how much I hated that white tile. Nearly everyday I thought, "I wish I just didn't have this white tile. This house could be so much nicer, if we just didn't have this white tile."

Guess what happened? Nothing. Everyday for three years I woke up to see that same ugly white tile. Do you understand why? I never talked about what I actually wanted. I targeted all my energy to what I didn't want. As long as I talked about white tile, even though I hated it, I kept getting white tile.

I detested having to mop the floors every single day. While

I was mopping those floors everyday, I was thinking how much I couldn't stand that white tile. All the thoughts I had about this white tile festered inside me. I could actually feel myself getting angry every time I looked at it. Isn't that ridiculous? All of that over some silly white tile!

The most interesting part to me is that I didn't understand why that white tile wouldn't go away. I thought I had made it very clear that I didn't want it. The inherent problem was that I didn't talk about what I wanted. I only talked about what I didn't want.

When you talk in terms of what you don't want, you keep getting what you don't want because you haven't substituted anything else. When I was a young parent I learned very quickly that telling a child, "Don't jump in that puddle," is the same thing as saying, "Jump in that puddle." The reason for that is the child probably hasn't even thought of jumping in the puddle, until you put the idea in his head. It's far better to focus on the true want. In actuality, your real desire is for the child to walk around the puddle. Therefore, to get what you want in that scenario, you have to say something like, "Here, walk around the puddle like I'm doing." When you fail to say what you want, you get what you don't want because you fail to give a clear suggestion of what you want.

For the remainder of this day, I challenge you to carefully examine how you speak about what you want, and examine all of those with whom you come in contact. I'm certain you'll be amazed. I had always thought of myself as a very positive and upbeat person, but I could not believe how much I spoke in terms of what I didn't want, when I closely examined my speech and thoughts.

Once I consciously began voicing what I wanted without comparing it to what I didn't want, here's what I realized:

CARPE PHONUM ❯ Get What You Want

It is possible to say what I want by *just saying what it is that I want!*

 Although I might think that I am voicing my desires, I might actually be putting energy into exactly the opposite of what I desire.

 Whatever I place my focus on, I get.

 When I focus on what I desire in terms of positive words and images, I experience feelings of gratitude, joy, and excitement.

One Saturday afternoon, while my husband was playing his cello at a concert, I decided to move all the furniture around in our family room. There was a wall that divided the kitchen from the family room and it really broke up the flow of our house. We had often said, "if only that wall weren't there..." That afternoon, I decided to act as if the wall weren't there and to move the furniture the way I truly wanted it to be, wall or no wall.

When my husband arrived home, he asked, "What did you do?" I answered, "I decided to move the furniture in this room the way we really want it and to create the energy for that." Normally Jim can't stand it when I move things around, but this time he was so positive. Instead of saying how I didn't like it the way it used to be and that I wished the wall just weren't there, I only talked about what we wanted. Jim said, "Wow! This is great! You know, we really should get rid of this wall."

Before I knew it, he'd gone out to the garage and come back with a sledgehammer. I actually had to tell him to go upstairs and get out of his Nordstrom suit! By focusing on what I wanted and speaking of it in those terms alone, I faced absolutely no resistance. This guy was even going to tear down a wall while wearing his $800 suit! Two hours later, Jim had the wall completely knocked down. The next week he scheduled a flooring company to come in and show us samples of wood flooring. Two weeks after he'd knocked down that wall, we had new, beautiful wood flooring all throughout our downstairs.

For three long years I moaned and complained about the floor downstairs, but nothing changed. As long as I focused on how much I hated that white tile, I kept having ugly white tile to clean every day. When I simply changed my focus to what I desired, our downstairs began to transform instantly before my eyes. Never doubt the expediency of the Universe to give you what you want! Just be sure you ask for what you want instead of what you don't want.

Being is Action

You may be tired of hearing that you have to think positively if you want your life to go well. I believe there's a reason for that. We all know that thinking positively doesn't protect us from experiencing challenges. We can think positive thoughts about our sales business, but that doesn't get us to pick up the phone nor does it make all our prospects say yes to us. It isn't enough to think positive.

You can sit around all day and think about improving your business and getting rich, but just thinking about improving your business or getting rich won't improve your business or get you rich. You must couple action with that thinking. The way to mix action with thought is to be what you are thinking. Being is action.

Thoughts are important, but a thought fueled by emotions is electric. Electricity is a power source that causes bodies to attract and repel each other. Your state of being is like an electric current that attracts or repels what you're thinking. When you're in good state of being, you infuse your body with positive feelings. When you're feeling down and out, you infuse your body with negative feelings. The feelings you generate act as magnets that pull certain experiences into your life. If you really want to improve your business and your life, you can no longer sit on the sidelines and think positively how things will be better tomorrow, once you get around to doing what you want to do. You must "be" what you are thinking about now. Too often we all put "being" on hold.

You think you have to show improvement in your business before you can be excited, you have to feel courage before you can be courageous, you have to maintain an overflowing bank account before you can be rich, etc. In other words, you think you must have something before you can be something. But you don't need to wait for anything to be what you desire. In being excited about your business, you create the feelings that attract more excitement. In being courageous, you find the courage you've been waiting for. In being rich, you generate the wealth you've always desired. You can be happy, excited, courageous or rich in any moment by feeling grateful, and letting the feelings of gratitude enrich your soul.

I decided to start feeling good frequently throughout the day by looking around me and finding something that made me feel good. Here in Tempe, Arizona, which is just outside of Phoenix, you can see palm trees everywhere. When I look at palm trees, I feel like my heart is expanding. I feel as though I'm visiting some exotic resort whenever I look up and see them and I use them as a constant reminder to let myself feel good throughout the day.

One of the most important things you can do is find something that reminds you to feel good. Feeling good is a powerful state of being. When you are feeling good, it's so easy to feel excited and grateful because it is in that state that you create what you want. When you're creating what you want, it's impossible to feel badly.

I experienced the truth in that awhile back, when I went to a school musical in which our oldest daughter, Theresa, had a part. After the production was over, Theresa said something that really hurt my feelings. I decided to go to the car to wallow in my anger.

While pouting in the car, I quickly noticed how angry I felt and that I was feeling angrier with each passing moment. Then something incredible happened. A freeing thought managed to get through to me. "You could decide to feel good right now." At first I rebutted, "I don't want to feel good. I want to stay angry." Finally I picked myself up off that imaginary prison floor and began groping along the cell walls. I looked up and saw the gorgeous palm trees as they swayed magnificently back and forth on that stormy night. Within seconds I felt that swelling energy in my heart and I began to feel good.

Before I knew it, the prison walls disappeared, as the anger I had felt could no longer be detected. I suddenly found myself a free woman — free of the need to be angry, the need to be right, and the need to justify feeling unappreciated. When my daughter came to the car, I was able to calmly tell her what had hurt my feelings and she was able to explain how she'd never meant to hurt me. If I hadn't bothered to get myself in a state of feeling good, we wouldn't have been able to communicate in such a positive manner. By feeling good, I was able to create what I wanted — a loving relationship with mutual respect.

When you're feeling good, you're in a state that attracts what you want. When you're feeling badly, you're in a state that's attracting what you don't want. It really is that simple. That's why it never serves anyone well to wallow in anger, pity, discouragement, frustration, or worry. In any of those states you are not being what's necessary to attract what you desire. The electrical current you generate in those destructive emotional moments repels the very things you deeply desire to have or experience.

Although I don't advocate waiting around until you feel courageous to take action (since you're never going to feel courageous until after you've taken action), I do believe that deliberately thinking about things that make you feel good is a form of action. In other words, being is action. That's why it's so important to be what you desire even before you have the courage, the confidence, the comfort, the time, the money, etc. In being what you desire, you attract more of what you desire. Let the false self rage about the ways you can't move forward in your life because of this or that. It stops screaming every time you walk past it calmly and take steps in the direction it thinks are too difficult for you. In this process of removing the illusion-ary shackles of your captivity, you discover how your business and your personal development are united.

The reluctance you feel to pick up the phone will greet you everyday, just as those trouble thoughts are there to greet you daily. You can't end call reluctance any more than you can stop those trouble thoughts from chattering. That's the seeming rub, isn't it? You hope the call reluctance and those trouble thoughts will go away, once you finally make some of those tough sales calls. But they don't. The key isn't to try and stop call reluc-tance or the trouble thoughts. The secret is to not let either of them stop you. You accomplish this by being who you want to be no matter what those trouble thoughts suggest.

What you have to continually remind yourself is that sales call reluctance is nothing but an illusion of those trouble thoughts. It doesn't have any redeeming qualities. It only seems real because you believe it is. The only way to see its illusion is to pick up that phone and call your prospect. This action alone reveals the lie of call reluctance. Every time you "Carpe Phonum," every time you seize the phone, even while you feel reluctant, even before you have the courage, you understand more thoroughly how those trouble thoughts always rage that you can't, when in reality you can.

Those haunting voices that tell you how you feel too afraid, that you need more time to prepare, that you'd be better off to call later — those voices have the appearance of a big prison door surrounded by huge evil guards. Your freedom will never come by trying to find a way to make that prison door with its guards go away. Every time you try that, a few more guards show up around the prison door. Your daily freedom comes from waking up, seeing the prison door with all its guards and remembering to simply walk up to the door, gently push it open and walk right past the guards. Oh yes, they'll rage, "What? You're walking past us! What?" But that's all they do.

Freedom from call reluctance doesn't come from making call reluctance go away. Freedom from call reluctance results from call willingness. Even while the guards of call reluctance do their best to appear haunting, they will step aside as soon as you do just one little thing... Carpe Phonum!

About The Author

Tammy Stanley

Tammy Stanley is a highly entertaining and informative speaker who delivers substance rich presentations. Attendees of Tammy's presentations leave with clarity and wisdom, joy and vigor, and the ability to take immediate harmonious action.

Tammy worked for 15 years in the fashion industry as a Senior Executive Sales Manager with Weekenders USA, a woman's direct sales clothing business. Company policies restricted any form of advertising other than "word of mouth."

Having only her voice as a form of marketing, Tammy built a 1.4 million dollar retail business in three years. In 1996 she received her company's President's award based on attitude, personal and unit sponsorship, and sales.

Tammy Stanley is passionate about education and business. She has worked in sales and sales training since 1990. She is the CEO of The Sales Refinery, which provides strategies to build company image inside and out through vocal marketing strategies and sales training.

As a family woman, she has been married to her husband Jim for over 20 years. They have four extremely active, talented and intelligent children.

Tammy's enthusiasm for life and business is contagious. Through her depth of analysis, her comfortable self-revealing style, and her captivating personal story telling she inspires her audience to take action.

Meeting Planners!

Most call reluctance programs start from the premise that once sales professionals have a good opening script and learn how to overcome objections, Sales Call Reluctance® will become a thing of the past. In other words, good sales training cures Sales Call Reluctance®.

Sales managers are then faced with choosing from the hundreds of different sales training programs available. Which sales training philosophy will work best with one's company, which are too simplistic, which are too complicated? Sales managers can't deny that the trained will always outperform the untrained, but their people are tired of hearing the same old thing over and over again.

Carpe Phonum offers an irresistible change from the traditional sales training programs. Before talking about telephone scripts and objection handling, it is essential to discuss what truly trips up more sales professionals than anything else... the voice inside their own heads! Always the biggest obstacle in any sales professional's career is himself/herself. When sales professionals learn how to get that critical player inside their own head out of their way, the potential is truly unlimited.

The implementation process of Carpe Phonum is simple and fast because it is a no-nonsense approach that can not be ignored or forgotten. Results come immediately. The realization that waiting to call prospects is the most destructive force in any sales professional's business motivates your salespeople to seize the phone now and cease waiting.

At this point you are probably wondering what is the best way to introduce Carpe Phonum to your sales organization. There are several options because different organizations have different needs. The current options are:

This Book or Audio Series

Carpe Phonum is a powerful book because salespeople relate very well to the different scenarios I describe. It is obvious that I did not read a few books and then put together a few ideas that sounded good in theory but fail to actually work in the real world. Carpe Phonum is the result of being in sales myself for most of my adult life and experiencing the constant trickery of the trouble thoughts of sales call resistance. Past clients confirm that they listen to it on the drive to work to get mentally tough and prepare themselves to "seize the phone" and call prospects right when they get to the office.

But, this book is not just for salespeople. All people relate to that little voice that constantly clamors for attention but never does anything to improve one's situation. In that sense, Carpe Phonum is for everyone who is a part of the sales process, be it product specialists, managers, marketing specialists, customer service personnel, or salespeople.

Carpe Phonum Keynote

To say that this speech was designed to assist sales professionals overcome sales call reluctance fails to convey the power and magnitude of "Carpe Phonum." Participants leave not only motivated; they leave incapable of returning to self-sabotage without catching themselves in the act! Watch your sales force grow mentally tough as Tammy takes them on a journey all around the necessary bases to reveal how to get to home plate and score sales day after day, week after week, month after month.

Take Action!

If you've enjoyed reading Carpe Phonum, then you will definitely enjoy putting my Carpe Phonum ideas to work in your business. When sales people learn the illogicality and futility in waiting, they likewise begin to see the absolute practicality in taking action now as opposed to later.

BEWARE if you just heard a little voice tell you to put this off until a later time in the future. That's the same misleading voice that tells your sales professionals to wait for a better time to call. What could possibly be a better time to increase company productivity than the present moment?

Isn't it time that your sales force stopped waiting to make calls and started seizing the phone? **Call The Sales Refinery to book Tammy as your keynote speaker at you next convention!** **480-775-4866**

More Audio Products for Direct Sales Consultants
order visit www.tammystanley.com

Attention - Direct Sales Representatives wanting a FULL calendar:

You Too Can Have Bookings Galore

Experience the overwhelmingly positive impact of getting
2 bookings from every show:

> Why you actually want objections from your prospects
> Three simple keys to handling objections
> How to melt any prospect's resistance to book a show
> How to subliminally prepare your prospects to want to
  book a show
> The one thing that transforms you from a pushy sales
  person to a welcomed friend

— · — · — · — · — · — · — · — · — · — · — ·

Say What You Do in a Manner that Attracts Attention!

Powerful Prospecting... Potent Results

Just some of the techniques you learn from this program:

> The top way to articulate a masterful message that holds any
  prospect's attention
> How to turbo-charge your marketing with "the slightest edge"
  principle
> How to impress your prospects on a subconscious level
> Why you must unleash your influence in 42 words and how to
  accomplish that
> Specific techniques to speak outside the box of mediocrity

— · — · — · — · — · — · — · — · — · — · — ·

Say What You Do in a Manner that Attracts Attention!

Maximizing Customer Retention and Sales

Just some of what you will learn in this audio:

> The most overlooked way of increasing your sales
> Why and how most direct sales consultants leave hundreds, if not
  thousands, of dollars on the table
> The most innovative strategies to keep customers buying from you
  again and again
> The top 7 most common marketing mistakes
> Promotions that get customers rushing to your events

Attention Direct Sales Leaders!

Do you ever feel like you have heard everything there is to hear about direct sales? Are you tired of hearing the same thing over and over?

If you want fresh ideas to inspire your sales team to the next level, you cannot afford to miss Tammy Stanley's series of *Get Results NOW*. Tammy's marketing know how and unique insights combined with her 15 years of direct sales experience at a high leadership level make for a day of training that ignites you and your team into action.

"Tammy gave me much insight into how people think and how it relates to running a successful business. I received many AH-HAH moments, and her full day seminar was worth every penny in 1 hour."
-Dina Buckley

"Using many of your techniques I was able to book 13 parties in 2 days."
-Teresa Benke

"30 years in the direct sales business, many years of training, seminars, books; no one has ever made more sense or made me laugh with her enthusiasm, passion, and directness than Tammy Stanley."
-Laura Law

Hosting a *Get Results NOW* workshop is easy. Tammy has a unique system in place to assist you in the set-up and promotion, and she removes all the monetary hassles by collecting all the registrations through her website, allowing you to put all your energy and focus into your team.

To learn more and to schedule a *Get Results NOW* workshop in your area, call The Sales Refinery at 480-775-4866